Glimpses of
South Florida History

Glimpses of
South Florida
History by Stuart McIver

FLORIDA FLAIR BOOKS
Miami, Florida

Designed by Bernard Lipsky

Printed and bound by Rose Printing Co., Tallahassee, Florida

Typography by Set-To-Fit, Inc., Miami, Florida

Manufactured in the U.S.A.

For Wallace and Virginia

Contents

Foreword by Charlton W. Tebeau *9*

Preface by John Parkyn *11*

PART ONE
The Way We Lived *15*

PART TWO
The Way We Worked *43*

PART THREE
The Way We Played *61*

PART FOUR
Events, Cataclysmic and Mundane *77*

PART FIVE
People Great and Small *104*

PART SIX
Scoundrels, Scandals and Scams *136*

PART SEVEN
Pipe Dreams and Nightmares *150*

PART EIGHT
Rooms With a View Historical *170*

Index *191*

Foreword

I confess to an absorbing interest in the study of grass roots history, of the beginning and early development of communities. Call it a romantic interest in a time when life was simpler and less hurried if you like. I believe it is more than nostalgia, rather it is an important way of finding out about ourselves and our surroundings.

What brought the first Indian inhabitants here? South Florida is one of the few places in the United States where Indians found they could live the year round without planting crops or storing food. There is ample evidence of that Indian heritage around us.

A century ago, a few remaining Indians lived in this region. The natural setting was little changed when the earliest white settlers began to arrive into the coastal areas of South Florida. The railroad reached Miami in 1896 and spurred more rapid growth. The real estate boom and bust, the 1926 hurricane, the depression in Florida, the Great Depression, and the advent of the second World War, all but stopped further development. Today's South Florida is mostly a product of the last four decades.

Very little of the wilderness that was South Florida remains. Only the seas around us and the threatened but unconquered Everglades bear any resemblance to our former natural surroundings. Are we also losing our historical past?

Stuart McIver has lived in this region for most of the years in which South Florida has been transformed into a vast metropolitan community with worldwide interests and connections. McIver's interest in South Florida's past history and his subsequent research have led him all over the area, from large, growing cities to sleepy, forgotten towns. In this book, he captures in an easy, entertaining style, the elusive, human side of South Florida history, mainly before the four formative decades.

The sum effect of his labors is to preserve and give greater understanding and appreciation to the historical past of a unique area of the world which offers such great appeal to so many people.

CHARLTON W. TEBEAU
Professor Emeritus and
Past Chairman of the History Department
University of Miami

Springfield, Georgia *August 1988*

Preface

On October 2, 1983, *Sunshine* made its debut as the weekly magazine of the *News/Sun-Sentinel*. Like most premiere issues, the first *Sunshine* was something of a shot in the dark – a tentative stab at capturing the interests of what (given South Florida's demographics) was bound to be a diverse and demanding readership.

The cover story in that first issue focused on the search for "Broward's Most Beautiful Woman." There was also an article on a teacher turned drug dealer, a fashion spread, a gossip column, a humor column and a diary of upcoming events. And tucked away on a single page, a little story on a 1920s rum runner named James Alderman – the only man ever legally hanged in Broward County. The title of the story was "The Way We Were", its author was Stuart McIver.

Like all magazines, *Sunshine* has adapted over the years to the preferences of its readers. New features have been introduced, old ones dropped. Of all the bylines that appeared in that first issue, only one remains as a regular contributor: Stuart McIver.

Why has "The Way We Were" maintained its popularity for so long? It is, after all, a history column – not the most obvious candidate for longevity in a restless and transient region such as the Gold Coast. I believe the answer lies in McIver's obvious love for his home state, his encyclopedic knowledge of his subject and his sense of what is likely to interest that mysterious creature, the "average reader."

It is a personal pleasure, then, for me to introduce a selection of Stuart McIver's best columns from *Sunshine*. They are shining examples of that rare combination: good history and good entertainment. To newcomers to South Florida, they will tell much about the area in which they have chosen to live; to old-timers, they will tell much that they probably never knew.

JOHN PARKYN
Editor
Sunshine Magazine
June 1988

Glimpses of
South Florida History

PART ONE

The Way We Lived

The First House on Hypoluxo Island

Generally speaking, a shipwreck is bad news. Not so for Hannibal Dillingham Pierce, who settled on an island near the south end of Lake Worth in 1873.

Pierce had worked the gold fields of Australia, gone whaling in the South Seas, fought for the Union forces in the Civil War and later was a scout in the Indian wars.

Having spent a fair amount of his life outdoors, Pierce wanted his family of three properly sheltered in a sturdy wooden house. But finding wood on a Florida coastal island was no easy task. The only real source of decent building materials was the beach. The boards washed ashore when ships broke apart in the Atlantic.

Pierce would cross over to the barrier island, later to become Palm Beach, and beachcomb for timbers. When he found the water-logged pieces of wood, he had to drag them over the ridge on the barrier island and raft them over to his island in the lake.

It took him many weeks to finish his tiny dwelling, consisting of an 18-by-24-foot room downstairs and an attic topped by a roof of palmetto fans.

A week or so after Pierce completed the house, Mrs. Pierce asked an Indian what his tribe called the lake. "Hypoluxo," he said. So the settlers decided to call their part of the lake Hypoluxo Island.

In later years, Pierce's homestead would become the site of the home of Col. Jacques Balsan and his wife, the former Consuelo Vanderbilt who for a time was also the Duchess of Marlborough.

And more recently, it was the location of the ritzy Manalapan Club – a far cry indeed from the days when the land held just a two-room house with a palmetto roof and a pile of stones in front to serve as a stove.

The Pierce home on Hypoluxo, ca. 1874. *(Historical Society of Palm Beach County)*

Building South Florida's First School

One evening in May 1885, the women who lived along the shores of Lake Worth met to discuss a mutual problem. There wasn't a single schoolhouse in all of Dade County, which in those days stretched from the Upper Keys to Stuart.

In 1936, Hattie Gale, who would become the county's first schoolteacher, recalled: "When women want to raise money, they organize a sewing society...The Ladies Aid Society came into existence with Mrs. R.B. Moore as first president. All through the long summer and fall they held their meetings at the homes of various members. This weekly gathering grew to be quite a social event, something to be looked forward to. But the object was never lost sight of and fingers were busier than tongues."

With their sewing, members of the Ladies Aid Society set about to earn enough money to buy a lot on North Lake Trail, in a community that would become Palm Beach. Dade County agreed to give the school district $200 for lumber to build a 22-by-40-foot building. The lumber was shipped from Jacksonville by schooner without charge. A man named George Lainhart supervised the construction, which involved virtually every able-bodied man who lived on the lake. If you couldn't handle a needle and thread, you wielded a hammer.

While the men were building the school, the women kept right on sewing. By the time the school was completed and painted red, the Ladies Aid Society had stockpiled a plentiful supply of garments for sale.

So the community held a fair at the new schoolhouse, taking full advantage of the winter tourists, who usually had more money than year-round residents. The year's work yielded a balance of $226.40 – more than enough to pay the school's start-up costs.

In May 1886, on a Monday morning, Hattie Gale opened the doors for seven students ranging in age from 6 to 17. Within a few days five more children were added to the roster, bringing the student body to 12. Among the group was Guy Bradley, who was later to be murdered by poachers at Flamingo in 1905, after he became the first Audubon Society game warden assigned to protect the birds of the Everglades.

The children sat at a rough table, built from scraps left over from construction of the schoolhouse. There were no blackboards, and the school books consisted of whatever books could be rounded up.

"For three months teacher and pupils worked and played together," Hattie Gale later wrote. "There were lessons learned by all, and some were not in books. The teacher was teaching for the first time, and it was the first school some of the pupils had ever attended."

It was, she added, "pleasant to think how largely it was a labor of love."

The old schoolhouse still stands, but it was moved to Phipps Park in Palm Beach. And it is still red.

Teacher Hattie Gale in doorway of first Dade County school, ca. 1896. At far right is Guy Bradley. (*Historical Society of Palm Beach County*)

Pioneers Among the Palms

Long before Henry Flagler brought his railroad to South Florida, a small colony of settlers lived a peaceful if primitive life on a sandy barrier island which would someday become famous as Palm Beach.

They settled along the west side of the island, along the shores of Lake Worth. In fact, in the 1870s and early 1880s, the whole area was called Lake Worth or sometimes Lake Worth Country.

A group of 13 persons, all related and all from Illinois, reached the lake in 1876 and staked out homesites. Land was cheap. The E.E. Geer family bought 40 acres for $50. Ten years later they sold it for $10,000 to R.R. McCormick for a winter home. Seven years later McCormick sold it to Flagler for $75,000 as a site for the world's largest resort hotel, the Royal Poinciana.

Except for an occasional hurricane or a bear strolling through the front yard, those early days lacked excitement. A shipwreck in the winter of 1878 proved a welcome break in the island's routine.

A Spanish brig, the *Providencia,* bound for Cadiz, washed ashore, loaded with coconuts from Trinidad. H.F. Hammon (who would later found a town called Hammondville which still later became Margate in Broward County) and Will Lainhart claimed the wreck and proceeded to sell the coconuts for two-and-a-half cents apiece.

Several of the families living on the island bought large quantities of the nuts and planted them on their properties. In less than a decade that wild planting binge would transform a sandy barrier island into "Palm Beach."

Life in those days was not without hardships. Panthers and wildcats ate the settlers' chickens, and snakes ate the chickens' eggs. In the poor, sandy soil of Palm Beach, farming was a difficult task. But the sun shone, the breeze came in off the ocean, and game and fish were plentiful. In a remarkable memoir of the pre-Flagler era, *Pioneer Life in South Florida,* Charles W. Pierce, who lived on Hypoluxo Island in the lake, wrote:

"When the first settlers came to the lake they found the woods fairly alive with game. Bears were plentiful in the beach hammocks and deer could be found everywhere, as well as wildcats, coon and possum, and an occasional panther. Wild turkeys were also fairly numerous, as were ducks in the winter time...

"Alligators were almost as plentiful in the lake as the fish, and there were some crocodiles and leatherback turtles...Nearly every settler had a gun and knew how to use it for procuring fresh meat."

The early settlers held picnics on the lake, celebrated Thanksgiving with turkey shoots and gathered together for community Christmas parties. They also had dances with music supplied by such nifty groups as the Hypoluxo String Band, whose members included the young Charles Pierce and Guy Bradley, who would later become the first Audubon warden killed in the line of duty.

In 1886 the settlers on the island petitioned the government for a post office. By this time the island looked like one huge coconut grove, so they suggested the name Palm City, not realizing that the name had already been taken by another Florida town. Pick another, the postal authorities said.

The name they picked was Palm Beach.

Lake Worth, ca. 1880, looking east towards Palm Beach. *(Historical Society of Palm Beach County)*

Taking a Six-Bit Ride on the Celestial Railroad

It started life as the Jupiter & Lake Worth Railway. And if people had continued calling it the J & LW, its brief days of semi-glory would by now be all but forgotten.

Luckily for the little seven-and-a-half mile railroad, a writer for *Harper's New Monthly Magazine* wrote about it in 1893, dubbing it the "Celestial Line." The writer, Julian Ralph, felt that the J & LW was too earthbound a name for a railroad that stopped at Jupiter, Venus, Mars and Juno.

So, the line became the "Celestial Railroad" and it remained a fond memory long after it had crashed into bankruptcy.

The line began operations in 1889, connecting Jupiter on the Indian River with the settlement of Juno on the north shore of Lake Worth. Way stations were Venus and Mars, neither of which flourished. Venus had a population of one man and two cats.

The line ran between what is today's Federal Highway and A1A, starting near the present-day Suni-Sands Mobile Home Park in Jupiter and ending near the Twelve Oaks Condominium.

The Celestial Railroad was a tiny branch of the Jacksonville, Tampa and Key West Railroad Company. The JT&KW ran from Titusville down the Indian River to Jupiter through its subsidiary, the Indian River Steamboat Company.

At Juno, the railroad connected with the steamer *Lake Worth,* which could then take passengers south to Palm Beach, Hypoluxo and Lantana. Unfortunately, connections were erratic.

The railroad made two trips a day. Passengers paid 75 cents one way for a 30-minute train ride. In 1891 the line added a second passenger coach. It also owned three freight cars but never more than one engine.

The Tropical Sun, published in Juno, frequently blasted the line for its bad service and poor station accommodations on the Indian River wharf and the Lake Worth docks.

What kept the line in reasonably good favor with the communities it served were its employees on the railroad and at the wharfs. The most popular man on the line was Blus Rice, its jovial, chatty engineer.

Rice had a rare skill. He is said to have been able to toot *Dixie* on the train whistle, even though it had only one tone. Rice, a mighty hunter, "leased" his hunting dogs to passengers who alighted from the train along the right-of-way and hunted for a while, returning to the train later when the engineer tooted for them.

The coming of Henry Flagler's railroad to the Lake Worth area ended the era of the Celestial Railroad. Its rolling stock was sold at public auction in Jacksonville in June, 1896.

Dora Doster Utz, of Jupiter, who played on the locomotive as a girl, wrote years later about the end of the line:

"There was something sad about how quickly the little stops along the Celestial right-of-way were abandoned. The jungle and the underbrush were fast claiming the right-of-way and the sorrowful call of the mourning dove seemed to sound a requiem to its passing."

The Celestial Railroad, engineer Blus Rice, center left. *(Bessie Wilson DuBois Archives)*

Building Your Own Railroad

It ran only 14 miles, and was propelled not by a steam engine but the front half of a Ford. Nevertheless, the Deep Lake Railroad was a South Florida version of *The Little Engine That Could.*

In 1917 it hauled 17,000 boxes of fruit from the grove at Deep Lake Hammock south to Everglades City, clearing the track of panthers and bears with a warning bell.

Deep Lake Hammock was 300 acres of relatively high land, near one of the homes used by Chief Billy Bowlegs and his band during the Third Seminole War.

After 1900, Walter Langford and John M. Roach bought the hammock, cleared 200 acres and planted them in Marsh seedless grapefruit. They figured that by the time the trees matured some form of transportation would be available.

By 1913, Langford and Roach had given up on public transportation. If they wanted a railroad, they were going to have to do it themselves.

Rails and rolling stock were shipped into Everglades City. From there the pair started the roadbed toward the hammock. The railroad was cut through the Big Cypress Swamp, along a rambling, ungraded route. George Storter, Sr., drove the first spike.

In a wilderness, even a small railroad excites interest. The *Key West Journal* in 1915 speculated that Deep Lake might someday be extended all the way to Cape Sable and from there over a 50-mile causeway to Key West.

Key West's dream never came true, but the little railroad had a few moments of glory after Barron Collier bought the Deep Lake property. Collier rebuilt the road, brought in steam locomotives and used the line for logging operations. Eventually, it wound up as part of the Atlantic Coast Line.

The Deep Lake Railroad, ca. 1913. *(Collier County Historical Museum)*

Poling to Frank's: A Cultural Exchange

They must have looked like an armada coming down the river. Sometimes, in the 1890s, as many as 150 Seminoles, poling dugout canoes and flat-bottomed boats, would arrive at Frank Stranahan's Trading Post on the New River to sell their pelts, hides and vegetables.

From their camps and villages along the river or on the hammocks in the Everglades, the Indians would venture forth into the Glades and the Big Cypress Swamp to hunt for about six weeks. When they came back home, they collected their skins, assembled their families, donned bright calico garments and moved down the river to Stranahan's.

Today, the Stranahan House is a museum located on the north shore of the New River east of Third Avenue. But in those days, it was a center of colorful international commerce.

The hunter, who was the head of the family, poled the canoe from the back. In front of him lay the hides he wanted to sell. The boat also carried his wife; children, cooking utensils and any other belongings he chose to bring. In the prow of the boat stood his dog, always the first ashore when the boat landed.

The Indians brought alligator skins, teeth and eggs, even live baby alligators; deer, raccoon, otter and fox skins, as well as corn, pumpkins, sweet potatoes, beans and bananas.

Stranahan, always scrupulously honest in his dealings with the Seminoles, paid in cash and sometimes the size of the payment was substantial. The average amount an Indian would receive was $50-$75 but, some mighty hunters could expect as much as $1,500.

Although the Indians couldn't read, they seemed to understand the U.S. monetary system. They knew within a few cents how much money they could expect for their skins.

Stranahan had come to the area in 1893 to run the New River Ferry and the New River Camp, which provided lodgings for travelers. Later that year he relocated to the site where the Stranahan House stands today. There he built his trading post, complete with boat slip for the Seminoles.

Once they arrived, the Indians stayed around Stranahan's place for as long as a week, sleeping on the grounds and on the porch of his home. He refused to sell them intoxicating drink and always made them stack their guns in his office until they were ready to return to their camps. He was firm in his dealings with them, but he earned their respect.

From Stranahan the Indians bought pots and pans, traps, shotguns, calico, hatchets, hammers and nails, jewelry, cigarettes (a commodity which they now sell), lard, butter and canned goods.

The Seminoles liked the music which emerged from Stranahan's phonograph, on which he played wax cylinder records, round like the canned goods they bought. They did not, however, like the sounds of voices on the phonograph.

According to one historical account, after hearing a recorded voice, a Seminole assembled his family and commanded: "Go. No like canned man."

Seminole canoes at boat slip at New River Camp, on west side of Stranahan House, ca. 1895. *(Fort Lauderdale Historical Society)*

Delray's Female-Powered Ferry

These days it's only tough crossing the Intracoastal Waterway when the drawbridge is up. Think of what it was like in the early part of the century in Delray Beach, when you were the drawbridge.

In those days, people who wanted to go to and from the beach had to use a flat-boat ferry. The larger of the two ferries was used for horses, mules and wagons. The smaller one was for people. Maximum load: 12.

The hitch was this. To cross, you had to step aboard the ferry, grab a chain connected to the other side and then tug until you finally drew the heavy barge to the distant shore.

It was less than back-breaking work, but it looked a bit on the rugged side for a young lady, fetchingly attired in a long white dress and wide, floppy hat.

Still, somewhere around 1902, an early photographer caught the local schoolmarm, a Miss Ewing, in the act. There she is, tugging away at the chain, while receiving no help at all from Mrs. Henry J. Sterling, or at the back of the barge, an English visitor named Mr. Crownover.

It's easy to see how Mrs. Sterling avoided the work. As the wife of one of the town's leading citizens, she simply outranked Miss Ewing. After all, these establishment-types usually avoid the heavy physical labor. That's how you get to be an establishment-type. But why wasn't Mr. Crownover giving us a bit of the chivalry for which Merrie Old England is noted? Come now, Mr. Crownover, simply not done. At least not in 1902.

Or are we seeing here an early surfacing of ERA thinking? Was Miss Ewing anxious to prove that a woman could ferry a boat every bit as well as a man?

They're all gone now, so we will never know why the heavy work fell to Miss Ewing. At any rate, it didn't do her any harm. She later married a prominent Delray farmer, John Schabinger. He may even have been attracted by the firm muscle tone that ferry towing can bring. Mr. Crownover stayed around, too, and married Mrs. Sterling's sister.

And, by 1910, nobody had to worry about who pulled the ferry across. A bridge over the Intracoastal at Atlantic Boulevard solved the problem once and for all.

Miss Ewing tugging the Delray Beach ferry, ca. 1902.
(Delray Beach Historical Society)

Steamboat Days in South Florida

Steamboat travel in South Florida was every bit as romantic as it was on the Mississippi. Passage on some of the early sternwheelers ranged all the way from high adventure to downright hardship. The colorful cast of characters included riverboat gamblers, blustering politicians, and even an occasional outlaw with a price on his head.

Take the case of the *Mary Belle,* the first steamer to operate from Kissimmee. The 47-foot sternwheeler offered cruises all the way down to Lake Okeechobee until it ran into a problem with a desperado named Bill Willingham. The *Mary Belle* had tied up at Grape Hammock to deliver goods to the outlaw. A quarrel broke out and Willingham pulled a knife. The crew overpowered him, tied him up and made arrangements to have him delivered by ox team to the authorities in Orlando.

But later, as the crew sailed south to Bassinger, they began to think about how Willingham's notorious gang might react to their display of civic spirit. So, rather than face reprisals, the crew simply sank the aging boat, and scattered.

The age of the steamboat in Florida lasted roughly 30 years until 1921. They were years which saw the beginnings of development in a wild and beautiful land. The steam age also featured a comical Florida version of the driving of the "golden spike" that connected America's railroads from the Atlantic to the Pacific.

Florida Gov. Albert W. Gilchrist was the instigator. Some 50 newspapermen from papers and wire services all over the country were riding with him as the steamboat *Thomas A. Edison* huffed its way up the Caloosahatchee River from Fort Myers to LaBelle. There they switched to the smaller *Queen of the Glades.*

The *Queen* carried the group up to Lake Okeechobee and then on to Ritta, on the south shore of the lake. There they spent the night at a hotel. The next day, April 26, 1912, Gov. Gilchrist was going to do a trick with a couple of coconuts that would symbolize what the much-ballyhooed trip was all about.

In 1906, the State of Florida had launched a massive program designed to drain the Everglades and thus pro-

Suwanee, ca. 1915. *(Fort Lauderdale Historical Society)*

Success cruised to Sanibel from Fort Myers. *(Fort Myers Historical Museum)*

duce dry, fertile farm land. The project had delivered less than it promised. As a result, papers all over the United States were running stories about the "Florida scandal."

Now after six struggling years, the first canal from the lower east coast to the lake had been completed. The governor wanted a critical press to know that something had finally been accomplished.

That morning the party reboarded the *Queen* and steamed into the North New River Canal. Out came the governor's coconut shells. One contained water from the Gulf of Mexico, the other water from the Atlantic. With ceremonial flourish, Gilchrist mixed the water from the two coconuts. By uniting the waters of the Gulf and the Atlantic, the governor was dramatizing Florida's first cross-state waterway. Now for the first time a boat could sail across Florida from Fort Myers to Fort Lauderdale.

To prove it, the party continued on down the narrow drainage canal through the Everglades, past sawgrass, tree islands and huge flocks of wading birds. When they arrived in Fort Lauderdale, they were greeted, reports say, by every man, woman and child in the little frontier town. To the governor's political eye, it added up to about 50 voters.

Overnight, the North New River Canal made Fort Lauderdale an important river port. Lake Okeechobee farmers and commercial fishermen packed vegetables and catfish down the canal for shipment via the Florida East Coast Railway to the cities of the northeast.

In December 1912, a momentous event occurred which brought a new and glamorous dimension to the New River port. The Menge Brothers Steamboat Company of Fort Myers inaugurated regular steamboat service between Fort Myers and Fort Lauderdale.

The Menge Brothers, sons of German immigrants, were a force to be reckoned with in South Florida steamboating. They owned and operated a fleet of five steamboats, including the *Thomas A. Edison*, three large barges, and six smaller launches for carrying passengers, freight and mail. The fanciest of the Menge paddlewheelers was the *Suwanee,* a 70-foot sternwheeler so elegant that she was used exclusively for passengers. (No one worried that *Suwanee* was a mispelled, lacking a second 'n'.)

Roundtrip fare on the *Suwanee* was only $25, including berth and meals in a dining room where white-coated waiters gave solicitous service. Because the ship was a doubledecker, its 32 passengers could count on an elevated view of the Florida scenery.

The Menge Brothers' brochure declared, "This route cannot be described. It is beyond description." Then the copy proceeded to describe it:

"The beauties are untold. The wild bird and game life has not been mentioned. The fishing has no parallel. The hunting is the best in the Union. The Seminole Indian still lurks in the forest abounding this route. It is a wilderness stretching for 200 miles from Gulf to Ocean. Nowhere else in America can such scenes be viewed except from the deck of the Steamer *Suwanee*."

Eva Bryan Oliver was one of the *Suwanee's* satisfied customers. More than most people, she could appreciate a good, roomy boat. At an important moment of her life, she had found herself struggling to keep her balance in a tiny row boat on the New River. The occasion was her wedding, the first ever recorded in Fort Lauderdale. She and husband Frank repeated their vows while standing in a cramped little boat. Frontier humor, 1902 style.

A decade later, as the wife of one of Fort Lauderdale's most prominent businessmen, Eva Oliver left behind a glowing account of a voyage on the *Suwanee:*

"Such a good trip it was," she wrote in the *Fort Lauderdale Free Press,* a long-defunct newspaper. "We had our meals in the boat. We left Fort Lauderdale late in the afternoon and arrived at the lake next morning. We began our stops at the different farms. At that time, sugar cane was three times as high as a person, and the vegetables and flowers were gorgeous. We came back down the canal in daylight and saw thousands of beautiful birds. It was a treat for tourists."

The *Suwanee* was indeed a treat for tourists, but not for long. The cross-state run lasted only two years before silting, water hyacinths and a shortage of paying customers made it impractical for a 70-foot sternwheeler to ply the canal's waters. Smaller steamers made the run for another nine years, before silting finally made the canal impassable.

South Florida steamboating had come about the hard way. It had its roots not in a network of naturally navigable rivers and lakes but in a series of drainage ditches.

The key was the big lake in the center of the state. The Seminoles called it Okeechobee, which means "plenty big water." Covering 730 square miles, it is the South's biggest lake. Unfortunately, no navigable streams flowed out of it to the sea, and the only stream of consequence that fed water into it from the north was the narrow, winding Kissimmee.

Because the rivers and canals were so narrow and winding, all the riverboats had to be sternwheelers. Sidewheelers, which were used in Central Florida, were simply too wide. The sternwheeler had another advantage, particularly along the meandering Kissimmee. Captains regularly backed up with sternwheelers so that the paddles could fan away hyacinths and silt and thus cut their own channels. The sternwheelers were known locally as "wet tails."

The Kissimmee's most colorful pilot was Clay Johnson, a gregarious, blasphemous, fiddle-playing captain who bore a strong resemblance to Mark Twain. If a dance was in progress on his route, Johnson would hop off his sternwheeler and play his fiddle. Then he would run his boat all night to make up for lost time.

Johnson had the reputation of being quite fond of the women along his route. Once, he grabbed one and tried to kiss her. Her hatpin scratched his face. When his wife met him at the dock, he said, "Oh, I just grabbed one of the girls and her hatpin stuck me." Naturally, his wife didn't believe him.

Faced with foul weather, Johnson was wont to shake his fist at the heavens, emit a stream of profanity and then fling a handful of coins into the wind to appease the water gods.

But the skipper would never have had a job to curse if it wasn't for Hamilton Disston, Philadelphia blueblood and heir to the Disston saw fortune. After buying 6,250 square miles of land from the State of Florida in 1881, Hamilton Disston became America's largest landowner. Since a substantial amount of the land was under water, Disston launched the state's first big drainage project from his headquarters in Kissimmee.

His crews widened and deepened the Kissimmee River and connected it to a chain of lakes so that a boat

Conrad Menge and his sternwheeler, *Uneeda,* 1924. *(Fort Myers Historical Museum)*

Clay Johnson's *Oscela. (Sunshine Magazine)*

could make its way to Lake Okeechobee. In addition, Disston dredged Three Mile Canal to connect the big lake with the Caloosahatchee River. This meant that steamers could finally sail from the Gulf up into the center of the state.

Later, in 1906, Gov. Napoleon Bonaparte Broward

Uneeda on the Caloosahatchee. *(Fort Myers Historical Museum)*

began a huge drainage project which connected the lake with the Atlantic and finally made cross-state navigation feasible. At one time, some 150 boats operated on Lake Okeechobee, taking advantage of a variety of routes.

There was a down-home flavor to those early steamboating days. The principal navigational aid on Lake Okeechobee was a flat-top cypress tree near Moore Haven. Captains delivered groceries to homes along their route and picked up produce for shipment to other points.

Boat landings lacked the glamorous international ring of the ports served by the transoceanic steamships. Instead of Liverpool, Southampton, Hamburg, and Barcelona, boats on the Kissimmee stopped at such points as Lone Cabbage, Lige Godwin's Farm, Hole in the Wall and Lofton's Woodyard.

Caloosahatchee landings included Coffee Mill Hammock, Prof Perry's and McCormick Still.

Most of the South Florida steamboats lacked the amenities of the *Suwanee*. In fact, traveling on some of the early sternwheelers ranged all the way from first class luxury to basic paddle-it-yourself

The first steamboat voyage from the Gulf to Kissimmee, a trip of only 200 miles, took 53 harrowing days. This was aboard the *Bertha Lee*, a 130-foot steamer from the Ohio River which found the shallow Caloosahatchee and the narrow, winding Kissimmee less to its liking.

Along the way, the crew had to build a dam to trap

enough water to float the boat free, get out from time to time to shovel a deeper channel, pull out cattails and water weeds to clear the way, and finally seek food from the Indians after their own supplies ran out.

That was the *Bertha Lee's* only trip up the Kissimmee. She was transferred to the Suwannee River for the run from Cedar Key to Branford. Later, while operating on the Chattahoochee River in Georgia, she hit a snag and sank. Most of South Florida's steamboats either sank or caught on fire.

As railroads and highways were built, South Florida boating began to lose its steam.

When the Hillsboro Canal was completed in 1913, the dredge crew members brought their girlfriends up from Fort Lauderdale to Deerfield, where they boarded the launch *Wanderlust* and cruised up the canal, across the lake and down the Caloosahatchee. They wound up their three-day trip with deep sea fishing in the Gulf.

Around this time, the Holland & Butterworth Company of Miami began advertising a $5 roundtrip voyage from Deerfield to Lake Okeechobee to view choice real estate.

Two other operators were Bill and Ben McCoy, who

Passing Thru at Okeelanta, 1919. *(Sunshine Magazine)*

Ad for Stone's Boat Line, 1921. *(Sunshine Magazine)*

ran motor launches up the West Palm Beach Canal and across the lake to Moore Haven, carrying tourists but no freight. After Prohibition, Bill McCoy changed jobs and became the era's most famous rum-runner, operating between the East Coast of Florida and the Bahamas. Because the booze he smuggled was so superior to moonshine, he became immortalized as the "real McCoy."

The last passenger steamboat from Lake Okeechobee to Fort Lauderdale made the trip on Christmas Day, 1921. At the helm of the *Passing Thru* was skipper Lawrence Will, self-styled "Cracker historian of the Everglades." In his *Okeechobee Boats and Skippers,* he wrote "...we kept chugging along and finally tied up in Fort Lauderdale at the foot of Brickell Avenue. It was 3:30 Christmas morning. I toted some of the lady passenger's goway bags to the hotel, and I reckon that was about the last time I've walked barefooted up the main street of Fort Lauderdale – well, the last time on a Christmas day at any rate."

The voyage of the *Passing Thru* was the end of an era that the *Suwanee* had ushered in, and the *Suwanee's* days in Florida were likewise coming to an end. In 1926, a killer hurricane sank the famous old ship at Moore Haven.

Belle of Suwannee takes on passengers. (Florida Photographic Archives)

Jupiter's Floating School Bus

How do you get to school when there are no roads for a school bus? If you lived in Jupiter in the early 1900s, you cruised to classes in a school boat on the Loxahatchee River.

The school boat was called the *Maine,* in honor of a U.S. battleship which won everlasting fame by getting itself blown up in Havana Harbor in 1898, thus setting off the Spanish-American War.

A 30-footer, the school boat came by its name naturally. At one time it had been a lifeboat on the *Maine.* Presumably it was not in service the day of the explosion.

The school boat started its run in 1903, piloted then by Dr. Charles Jackson, a homesteader on the north fork of the Loxahatchee. He was also the school's teacher, assisted by his daughter Mary until both of them moved to Coconut Grove in Miami, where Dr. Jackson became an Episcopalian clergyman.

The best loved of all the school boat captains was Doc Blanchard, whose name predated that of the Army football star by some four decades. Doc lived upriver with his sons Merle and Bertie. Doc rode at the helm where he could clang the bell, while Bertie operated the engine.

Doc and Bertie first collected the upriver children and dropped them off at the Florida East Coast Railway docks, close enough for them to walk to school. Next, they cruised farther east to pick up children living near the Jupiter Lighthouse and the inlet.

Doc ran a happy ship. The older boys whiled away drive-time by trolling for fish. The captain could afford to be tolerant. If they caught a fish, it usually wound up in his fish stew.

Entertainment was even supplied on occassion. One day when both he and Bertie were away on jury duty, Doc entrusted the boat to his father-in-law, an old timer named Graves who sported white hair and long white whiskers.

When the boat slammed too hard into the lighthouse docks, Old Man Graves toppled into the river. Fortunately, Captain Joe Wells, keeper of the lighthouse, managed to pull him out of the water, shaken up but unhurt.

A half-glass of whiskey and some dry clothes improved the old man's outlook dramatically. For the snickering students it had been quite a show — all part of getting a pioneer education on the river.

The Jupiter school boat. *(Historical Society of Palm Beach County)*

Pioneers Fiddled as Florida Grew

A century ago, South Floridians had no radios, stereos or tape players to soothe, or assail, their ears with music. It didn't matter to the pioneers. They made their own music. Sometimes they even created their own audiences.

Uncle John Cleminson of Jupiter used to play the violin for a team of mules. He drove the hack that delivered the mail from Jupiter to Juno in the 1880s. Much of the time he walked ahead of the team, sawing away on his violin. Author Marjory Stoneman Douglas dubbed him the "fiddling mailman."

When the Celestial Railroad took over the mail route in 1889, adding the starry towns of Mars and Venus, Uncle John lost his mule audience. But the new carrier did not neglect his music. Engineer Blus Rice, legend has it, used to toot *Dixie* on the train's steam whistle.

Meanwhile, Uncle John kept playing with the area's top musical group, the Hypoluxo String Band, which included more than strings. Cleminson tooted on the piccolo for the band which boasted an all-star lineup of Guy Bradley, first violin; George Lyman, second violin; Louie Bradley, cello; Henry Sanders, bass horn; Will Sanders, piano, and Charlie Pierce, cornet.

Guy Bradley would later become the first Audubon warden killed in the line of duty. His brother Louie was one of the first barefoot mailmen. Their mother, Mrs. Lydia Bradley, was a trained musician, skilled as a vocalist and a guitar player.

The Hypoluxo String Band played at dances at such varied halls as M.B. Lyman's new store in Lantana, the Palm Beach Yacht Club and Palm Beach's first hotel, the Cocoanut Grove. After a gig on Palm Beach, Pierce and the Bradleys would sail across Lake Worth to their homes on Hypoluxo Island and in Lantana at three a.m.

Georgian Jesse Malden was the area's first commercial hunter as well as its first fiddler. He played music commonly described as "backwoods tunes." The Hypoluxo String Band worked from such songbooks as *Howe's Beginner's Quadrille Band Book* and *White's Home Circle Orchestra.* Among the tunes they played were *The Girl I Left Behind Me* and *Home, Sweet Home.* At least one early musician, E.M. Brelsford, didn't think the tune made that much difference. He once advised Charlie Pierce:

"Time, time, just give them time, that's all they want. It doesn't make any difference what kind of tune you play, as long as it has the right time."

Uncle John Cleminson, ca. 1900. *(Bessie Wilson Dubois Archives)*

Fort Lauderdale's First "Party" Boat

In the late 1800s, a few modest dwellings and shacks graced the New River area that would one day be the site of Fort Lauderdale's poshest mansions. The first luxury housing to show up at the riverfront settlement wasn't even a house. It was a boat.

In 1896, Charles Barney Cory, heir to a New England wine and silk fortune, purchased a Mississippi River packet boat and had it refurbished. Total cost: $100,000, a staggering sum at the time.

Cory, who wintered in Palm Beach, docked his 90-foot houseboat near Frank Stranahan's trading post in Fort Lauderdale. The *Wanderer,* paneled inside with mahogany, contained 12 bedrooms, a magnificently appointed lounge, recreation rooms, the area's only piano, and a gun room which housed an arsenal of firearms as well as an elaborate collection of fishing tackle. Cory's guests on the opulent stern-wheeler included former President Grover Cleveland.

Cory, a bear of a man who sported a spectacular handlebar mustache, found great joy in the pursuit of wildlife. His study of animals, birds and fish produced a number of highly regarded books.

The other form of wildlife he enjoyed were shipboard parties that went on for days and usually recurred at two-week intervals. With the aid of his good friend, the noted American actor Joseph Jefferson, he was able to attract to the *Wanderer* a goodly supply of women described by envious townfolk as "wild young actresses."

The story goes that young Tom Bryan, destined to become one of the political pillars on which modern Fort Lauderdale would be built, learned the facts of life by rowing his boat out into the river and gazing in wonder at the carryings-on aboard the *Wanderer.*

The *Wanderer's* partying days ended in 1926, when one of the deadliest hurricanes ever to strike South Florida came roaring out of the Caribbean and smashed the boat. But it certainly wasn't the end of revelry on the river, as today's yachtsmen will attest.

The *Wanderer,* ca. 1896. *(Fort Lauderdale Historical Society)*

Planting the Seeds of Fort Lauderdale

When the founding fathers of Fort Lauderdale gathered to vote their town into being, they fit easily into a one-room schoolhouse. There were only 45 qualified voters.

Those first citizens thought small, not big, at their meeting on March 27, 1911. In debating the size of the town, the voters decided on one and one-half square miles, feeling that two square miles would be too large.

But no meeting was too small to generate controversy. In what must have been the first-ever protest about local politicians doing deals in secret, the area's only physician, Dr. Tom Kennedy, walked out of the incorporation meeting. According to the local newspaper, Kennedy claimed that, "The whole thing had been done wrong, that he did not believe in the secret Sunday morning meetings held without giving due notice to the people interested."

It was Reed Bryan, namesake of today's Bryan Homes restaurant, who formally proposed the city be named Fort Lauderdale. He then nominated vegetable grower William H. Marshall to be the first mayor. Marshall easily beat his opponent, Joe Farrow, 30 to 6.

Mayor Marshall's achievements set a dazzling standard for future politicos. He pushed for city ownership of the downtown riverfront, for seawalls along the fast-eroding banks of the New River, for the creation of the Everglades Drainage League, and for women's suffrage.

Marshall was re-elected mayor in 1912, and when Broward County was formed in 1915, he was elected to two terms as the county's first state representative. Many years later he was appointed to fill an unexpired term on the Fort Lauderdale City Commission, serving from 1947-1949.

In his private life, Marshall was an organizer of the First Methodist Church and president of the Dade County Bank. He lobbied in Washington for the Tariff Act of 1930 to protect vegetable growers in South Florida, and financed the education at Carlisle Indian School of Tony Tommie, the first Broward Seminole to seek the white man's schooling.

Born near Valdosta, Ga., in 1876, Marshall moved with his family to North Florida in 1884, then settled on the New River after being mustered out of the Army after the Spanish-American War. He became a major vegetable grower, the first in South Florida to sell his crops by mail order.

Years later Mrs. Marshall recalled her arrival in Fort Lauderdale on Dec. 31, 1909, a mere 15 minutes before the birth of 1910:

"It was a beautiful moonlit night. We left the train into the absolute silence and the wilds along the New River. We took a moment to view the reflection of the moon on the river, then turned to the sounds of music from the Stranahan home where a New Year's Eve party was in progress.

A lot of partying has followed on the New River since the night the Marshalls arrived.

Mayor William H. Marshall, ca. 1911. *(Fort Lauderdale Historical Society)*

On Chokoloskee, Each Man Was an Island

Head out across Alligator Alley, then drive south on State Road 29, past Everglades City, until you can't go any farther. You'll be on Chokoloskee Island, stepping-off point to the Ten Thousand Islands.

The island is less than 150 acres in size – yet it has seen more than its share of rugged individualists over the years.

Probably the first white settler in the area was Capt. Dick Turner, sometime in the 1870s. He had been a scout for the U.S. Army during the Third Seminole War, in the 1850s, and gave his name to the scenic Turner River, a stream highly regarded by today's canoeists.

C.G. McKinney, the man who would become the "Sage of Chokoloskee," came to the island in 1886. He started the island's first store and its first post office, and was widely known for years as a newspaper correspondent, given to a picturesque turn of phrase. Under his pen, mosquitoes became "swamp angels" and moonshine whiskey "low bush lightning."

McKinney's business policy was spelled out on his store's letterhead: "No Banking. No Mortgaging. No Insurance. No Borrowing. No Loaning. I must have cash to buy more hash."

For people who think today's schools are overwhelmed by problems, here's what McKinney wrote about the Chokoloskee School in 1924: "Our school-teacher...is going to give up her school today, it is too much for her nerves. She seems to be a nice refined body and we are sorry for her. She had a trying time here, but we can give her praise for her endurance. Maybe we don't need any school – we all know enough anyway. They seem to learn to chew tobacco, curse and drink booze at an early age and think their education is complete when they have these necessities ground into their topknots."

Joe Lopez was a Chokoloskee individualist of note. He was an active plume hunter – a trade that became increasingly difficult in Florida as state and federal laws began to halt the killing of egrets to provide feathers for women's hats. Joe and his sons went over to British Honduras (now Belize) to kill birds. They brought Joe back so ill that he had to be carried ashore on his bed. The mattress was stuffed with smuggled egret plumes.

The best known of all latter-day Chokoloskee figures was Ted Smallwood. He came to the island in the 1890s and operated the settlement's biggest store as well as its post office.

Because Chokoloskee Bay was so shallow, only the smallest of boats could make it in to his trading post. Without waiting for the Corps of Engineers, Ted just dredged a channel several hundred yards long from his dock out to deep water. His dock, incidentally, was the scene of the gunning down of Ed Watson by angry Chokoloskee settlers. Watson himself was a one-of-a-kind renegade, a man so feared that when he refused to surrender his gun, he was shot to death by an angry mob at Smallwood's.

A 1924 hurricane blew in Ted Smallwood's front door, moved four feet of water into his store and lifted it off its foundation. This was warning enough for Ted. He built pilings and raised his store eight feet, just in time to protect the property from the devastating September, 1926 hurricane.

A colorful man with a bushy, handlebar mustache, Smallwood lived until 1943. His daughter Thelma ran the store until her death four decades later. The old building still stands, but it is no longer operating as a store.

"In Thelma's will she left it to the park (Everglades National Park) or if we couldn't work it out, to the state," said her brother Glen Smallwood, in his seventies and still an active charter boat captain. "Pretty soon, we'll have it worked out."

Capt. Smallwood is confident that the old store his father built in 1917 will be preserved – a monument to the pioneering spirit of the Ten Thousand Islands.

Ted Smallwood in doorway of his store, ca. 1930. *(Historical Association of Southern Florida)*

A Hideaway at the End of the World

When the settlers at the tip of Cape Sable established a post office in 1893, they were told they had to give their settlement a name.

They considered End of the World. Instead, they picked a romantic, exotic name for their own personal hell-hole. They called it Flamingo, shortened on occasion to Mingo and lengthened on others to Fillymingo.

In the 1890s, flocks of the spectacular tropical birds were commonly seen in the Cape Sable area, although South Florida was at the end of the bird's range, so the name made sense. So did End of the World, since the Cape at that time was an isolated society populated mostly by people who were running away from something – the law, civilization, or maybe their wives.

When they reached the Cape, they knew they had arrived at the end of mainland Florida. There was nowhere else to go.

"Uncle" Steve Roberts came to Flamingo in 1901. He was born in Micanopy and his father is said to have laid out the town of Gainesville. Some say Roberts came south for his wife's health, some say for his own, since there were reports linking him with cattle rustling.

Whatever the reason, Uncle Steve stayed on and became Flamingo's power structure. With him he brought his five sons and three daughters, a population explosion in its own right, in a town of only a half-dozen families.

People at the Cape made their living fishing, raising sugar cane, making moonshine and smuggling. Uncle Steve was active in a number of these frontier pursuits. Though he was reported to be a plume hunter, two of his sons were Audubon wardens trying to stamp out the illegal trade.

One of the settlers' worst enemies were mosquitos. Stories abound that they they had been known to kill cows and mules left out for the night.

Every house was equipped with smudge pots and a palmetto fan. When you entered a Cape Sable shack, you brushed yourself off with the palmetto in a room called a "loser." It was where you were supposed to lose your mosquitos.

Most of the houses were built on stilts to guard against hurricanes or high tides from Florida Bay. Uncle Steve's home became the Roberts Hotel in 1915. His two-story house had four bedrooms upstairs for regular or transient boarders. Extra mattresses on the floor took care of overflow guests. The old hotel was destroyed by a hurricane in 1926.

Making syrup and moonshine whiskey from sugar cane was a major industry at Flamingo. In 1908, the cane was beseiged by a horde of rats. Uncle Steve's son, Gene, came up with an idea to save the town.

"Men," he told a gathering, "we've done everything we could think of to get rid of the rats, but it ain't done no good...These few cats we got here has done the best they can, but they can't eat but so many rats. So I say we ought to chip in and run down to Key West and buy up a whole bunch of cats and bring 'em here."

Gene took up a collection, then set sail for Key West. A sign reading "Will Pay 10 cents Apiece for Every Cat Delivered to this Dock" brought him a cargo of 400 cats to take back to Cape Sable.

"That 90-mile trip was the worst I ever made," said Gene.

The cats took one look at Flamingo, then disappeared into the wilderness. But they did wipe out the rats.

In 1922, a road was completed linking Flamingo with Homestead. Many hoped the town would blossom. Just the opposite happened. It lost population. People had found a way to get out. Now the town at the end of the world is a resort at the end of Everglades National Park.

The Roberts Hotel in Flamingo, ca. 1920. *(Historical Association of Southern Florida)*

The Wild, Wild Davie General Store

All that remains of the old store that once served as the heart of the Davie community is a grassy bank on the south side of the South New River Canal. Not even a trace of the foundation can be found.

Built in 1912, the galvanized iron building served as trading post, school, post office, ice house, dock and general meeting place for the agricultural community. Kids swam in the canal in front of the store, wary, of course, of alligators and water moccasins. And boat traffic moved in and out of the dock area at a time when the canal was the only "road" to Davie.

When Governor Napoleon Bonaparte Broward began his program to drain the Everglades, the second canal to be dredged was the South New River Canal, started in 1907. This opened up land for farming and led to the establishment of the first settlement on sawgrass land reclaimed through drainage.

The community was first called Zona, since many of the settlers came from the Panama Canal Zone where they had worked on the vast canal project. The name was later changed to honor R.P. Davie, a Colorado Springs land developer, who bought 27,500 acres of the reclaimed land.

In its earliest days, the canal-front store was known as Goodson and Ingle. Next it was owned by A.B. Lowe, first chairman of the county commission, and then by Ed Middlebrooks, who came to Davie from Georgia.

By the mid-1920s, talk of incorporation was in the air. As befits the town that later became the center for South Florida cowboys and home of an annual state championship rodeo, lawlessness was a major reason, as indicated by this letter from a Mrs. Middlebrooks to the Fort Lauderdale Chief of Police, in 1925:

"I want to ask you if you all can't let us have a good man out at Davie for protection. I declare the drunkenness and misbehavior in front of the store I can't stand and at times they try and do come in the store and cut up, then if anybody tries to get them out, then comes the trouble." She concluded, "I try to raise my boys right and they listen to me and I don't want to be bothered with such goings on."

The incorporation vote was held on Nov. 16, 1925. The vote was 28 for, two against.

The old store was torn down in the 1940s, still in surprisingly good shape, although it looked as though it was close to collapse even in its early days.

The Davie general store, ca. 1920. *(Fort Lauderdale Historical Society)*

One Thin Dime Bought Four Reels

Delray's first movie theater was the Bijou, where you could see "4 reels, extra fine show" for just 10 cents.

Those were indeed the good old days.

"I remember going to the Bijou as a boy," recalls Buster Musgrave, whose family moved to Delray from southern Indiana in 1923. "You could see a western and a serial on a Saturday afternoon and eat a bag of popcorn for a nickel.

"Kids would go there and eat popcorn and stomp their feet on the wooden floor. They made a lot of noise. Mrs. Tembrook was a fussy old lady. She really got after them for stomping their feet."

Mrs. Elizabeth Tembrook was owner and operator of the town's first theater and she ran it for close to two decades. Her husband, Frank, owned the adjacent Tembrook Building, renting out stores on the first floor and apartments on the upper floors.

The Bijou was Mrs. Tembrook's special project. Her husband was not involved in its operation but she did need additional help. To handle the projector, she hired a moonlighting member of the Delray Fire Department.

Conflicting accounts make it hard to pinpoint just when the Bijou was built, but it was most likely during the period just after the end of World War I in 1918. Certainly it had to be after 1914, the year electricity came to Delray.

The Bijou began operations in the days of silent movies, when title cards took the place of spoken dialogue and actresses batted expressive eyelids at the fascinated public.

Along the way, many changes, for better or worse, affected the workings of the Bijou. Sound found its way into the movies. Mrs. Tembrook for some reason decided the Roxy was a better name than the Bijou, but most important of all to the eventual fate of the Bijou/Roxy was the arrival in town of competition.

In 1925, John Hall built a handsome structure which he called the Delray Theater. Located across from the Colony Hotel on what is now Fifth Avenue, the theater was run by his son, Emmett.

By the mid-'30s, Mrs. Tembrook's old movie house was running out of steam. It was finally torn down, leaving only silver memories of a time when you could enjoy an "extra fine show" for just a dime.

Matinee at the Bijou, 1925. *(Delray Beach Historical Society)*

The Great Voyage of "Key West Billy"

Billy Fewel decided to see a little of the world beyond his tribal home in the Big Cypress Swamp. One of the places he wanted to visit was Key West, about 125 miles south.

But in the 1880s, it wasn't an easy trip to make, particularly since his only means of transportation was a dugout canoe, traditionally propelled by poling.

Billy had to travel first from the swamp west to the Gulf of Mexico. By working his way down the coast, he could make use of some protected waterways or at least stay close to land if bad weather developed.

However, from Cape Sable southwest to Key West the distance was nearly 60 miles across open water. That didn't stop Billy; somehow he made it. Perhaps he made use of a sail. Seminoles sometimes used them with dugouts.

At that point, his legendary feat earned him a new name – "Key West Billy." So great was his fame that a second – and highly unlikely – story surfaced that he had paddled his way over to Havana.

Key West Billy was the brother of another well-known Indian, Billy Conapatchee, the first Seminole known to have attended the white man's schools.

In his later years, Key West Billy lived in the Big Cypress southeast of Immokalee, in a camp with an unusual name. Billy called it Californee, but then, he was a cosmopolitan type.

The Indian agent, Rev. James L. Glenn, described it as " one of the most beautiful Indian homes that I have ever known." Billy shared the dwelling with his son-in-law, Wilson Cypress.

The home was built on high land surrounded with guava and banana trees. Glenn wrote about a 1928 visit, when the gracious old Indian was believed by the agent to have been more than 100 years old:

"Billy told us a story about his garden, which he did not believe any more than we believe our stories of good or ill luck. He said that the Indians say that if, after you cut the brush away, dig up, and fence a plot of land like this for a garden, if a young Indian maiden in her birthday dress passes through it in the wee hours of the night, the plot will be blessed with rich ground and plenty of corn, pumpkins, and other products."

Agent Glenn, being a man of the cloth, did not comment on whether "birthday dress" to Billy meant the same as the white man's "birthday suit."

Key West Billy, left, and Wilson Cypress at their spread in Californee. *(Fort Lauderdale Historical Society)*

Friends on the Wild Frontier

They were born the same year, 1886, in the wild frontier of southwest Florida. But they came from different worlds.

Frank Brown was the child of a white family reaching out to the Indians; Josie Billie was the child of a Miccosukee family reaching out to the white man.

Frank's father was a true Anglo, a native of Bristol, England. Starting from a base in Fort Myers, Bill Brown kept moving his trading post deeper and deeper into the Indian hunting grounds.

In 1901 he established his legendary Brown's Boat Landing on the western edge of the Everglades, 30 miles east of what is now Immokalee.

Josie's father was likewise a trailblazer, known both as Little Billy and Billy Conapatchee. He broke tribal law by attending the white man's school in Fort Myers. For this transgression, members of the tribe decreed that he should be put to death. He stayed out of sight for a year, until the killing fever passed.

Josie Billie inherited his father's thirst for learning. As a boy, he spent many hours at the home of his friend, Frank Brown. From one of the women at the Brown household in the Everglades he learned to read and write English.

Frank, in, turn spent weeks at a time with Josie's family, hunting throughout the Big Cypress. He came to know the swamp as no white man had ever known it before. Throughout his lifetime, he was a sought-after hunting guide.

Josie was married three times, and lived for a while on the Big Cypress Reservation. When the Tamiami Trail opened, he established a camp near Ochopee. As a young man, Josie was fond of whiskey, and in 1928 he stabbed an Indian woman to death during a drunken brawl. He was later found blameless by the tribe.

Josie's quest for self-improvement never stopped. He studied first to become a tribal doctor and in 1937 attained the honored position of medicine man and chief of the Miccosukees.

Sometime around 1943, Josie Billie became a Baptist convert. By 1946, he received his first formal schooling, attending the Florida Baptist Institute at the age of 60.

After his conversion, he became a teetotaler.

Both Josie and Frank, born in the days when Florida was a vast wilderness, survived into the age of color television, condominiums and space travel. Both died in their 80s.

They remained friends to the end.

Josie Billie, left and Frank Brown, ca. 1900. *(Florida Photographic Archives)*

Tony Tommie Goes to School

Back in 1913, Tony Tommie, a Seminole Indian, wanted to go to the white man's school, The tribe didn't like the idea. In the 1880s Billy Conapatchee had been placed under a tribal death sentence for attending school in the Fort Myers area.

James Rickard, Fort Lauderdale school principal, wasn't sure he could fulfill Tony's wish. For one thing, public schools in 1913 were segregated; mixing of the races just wasn't permitted. For another, there was the age problem. Tony would have to start in the first grade and he was already a teenager, somewhere between 14 and 18. No one knew for sure.

The third problem was even weirder. Since the Seminoles, unbowed after three wars with the United States, had never signed a peace treaty with Washington, young Tony Tommie had no legal status in the land of his birth.

Baffled, Principal Rickard referred the problem to the school superintendent, R.E. Hall, who in turn bounced it on to Lucian E. Spencer, special commissioner to the tribe. Spencer liked the idea and obtained $150 from the Bureau of Indian Affairs to cover the costs of sending Tony to school.

After preliminary tutoring, the young Indian entered the second grade. Instead of the knickers the other boys were wearing, Tony wore long trousers and the traditional Seminole shirt. He was barefooted. Despite differences, he became a popular student.

After he had completed his education, Tony decided to try his hand at the movie business. His first screen role, in 1919, came as a leader of a bloodthirsty band who were seeking to burn hero and heroine at the stake in the serial *The Great Gamble*. Next, he was engaged by screen director D.W. Griffith to hire local Seminoles for roles as South Seas natives in *The Idol Dancer*, a film Griffith was shooting in Fort Lauderdale.

Tony belonged to an important Seminole bloodline. His mother Annie Tommie was a highly respected medicine woman, and his nephew, Howard Tommie, would later become the tribe's chief.

Over the objections of many tribe members, Tony became a self-styled spokesman for the tribe. In Washington, he talked to officials about ending a war which had started in 1816. He sought benefits for his people. A Gulf coast Seminole leader, Ingraham Billy, denounced Tommie as "a fakir and traitor to his tribesmen."

Though Tony Tommie had started his tribe toward some sort of accommodation with a world pressing in on them from all sides, he didn't live to see much accomplished. In 1931, he died of tuberculosis.

Funeral services were conducted at the Dania Methodist Church. Then, Tony's body was taken about a mile south of the reservation and buried near a clump of palmetto bushes. Today, he is still remembered by oldtimers as the young Indian who tried to bridge the gap between two different, and often hostile, cultures.

Annie and Tony Tommie. *(Fort Lauderdale Historical Society)*

The Parson of Porgy Key

Israel Lafayette Jones, a pioneer black settler of Miami better known as "Parson Jones," had such a high regard for the Knights of the Round Table that he named his first son King Arthur, his second Sir Lancelot.

Jones and his family lived on Porgy Key in lower Biscayne Bay. When the birth of his second child was eminent, Jones tried to sail his wife to the office of the pioneer Miami physician, Dr. James M. Jackson. They didn't make it in time, and Lance was born in a boat on Biscayne Bay in 1900.

Jones came to South Florida from North Carolina. Born in Raleigh, he later moved to the state's major port, Wilmington. There he became a stevedore, acquiring considerable skill in the handling of small boats.

An adventurous man, he journeyed to Florida. In Coconut Grove he met Ralph Munroe, boat designer, founding commodore of the Biscayne Bay Yacht Club and agent for Waters S. Davis, a Texan who owned most of Key Biscayne. Jones asked for a job.

"What do you know about operating small boats?" asked the commodore.

"I sailed them around Wilmington," replied Jones.

"Come back tomorrow and we'll test you in a boat."

The next day Commodore Munroe tested Jones in a small fishing smack. Parson Jones passed easily. He got the job.

By 1897, Jones, one of early Miami's most successful black businessmen, had saved enough money to buy Porgy Key for $300 – roughly $5 an acre. There, he did a little of everything. He raised key limes, hired out as a fishing guide and even worked for awhile on a railroad that operated on Elliot Key.

Parson Jones also had a reputation as a philosopher. Commodore Munroe used to sail down to Porgy Key several times a year just to sit around and reminisce with him. Another frequent visitor was Kirk Munroe, a popular Coconut Grove author of boys' books. Jones's sons were avid readers of Kirk's books.

Porgy Key is now part of Biscayne National Park. Lance, the last of the Joneses, sold it to the U.S. Park Service but was allowed to live out his days on the little key that has always been his home and his base of operation when he worked as a bonefishing guide. His description of life today on Porgy Key: "Lonely, but not lonesome."

Israel "Parson" Jones, ca. 1900. (*Historical Association of Southern Florida*)

Old Time Religion, LaBelle Style

On revival day, the whole town of LaBelle gathered by the river, just as Christians had in Biblical times.

When the Reverend Oscar Roberts came to town for a day of sermonizing and baptizing, a big tent was erected near a boat house on the Caloosahatchee River. In 1920 LaBelle's population was about 300, and the townsfolk would line the riverbanks, some just to watch, others to experience a religious conversion.

LaBelle, some 30 miles west of Lake Okeechobee, was the seat of Hendry County. Roberts, a Baptist missionary from nearby Wauchula, where he raised cattle, didn't limit his revival meeting to Baptists. But he reserved dunking in the river for those of his faith.

Baptism was total immersion in order to wash away one's sins, cleanse the soul, and complete admission to the church. Many other faiths performed baptism symbolically by sprinkling water on the head.

Alvah Burke, in his nineties, a former river boat pilot who knew the Rev. Roberts as a young man recalls:

"He didn't baptize Methodists. They believed in sprinkling. Oscar Roberts didn't believe in sprinkling. It wasn't baptizing if you weren't baptized in the river. No place in the scriptures that gives sprinkling for baptizing."

If Methodists, Presbyterians or Episcopalians, all of whom had churches in LaBelle, wanted to be baptized, Roberts referred them to their own preachers.

After the baptisms, everyone returned to higher ground and enjoyed a picnic dinner. Members of all faiths mingled freely.

"People got together better then," says Burke. "They don't bunch up now like they used to. Used to go miles for any kind of public meeting."

The Baptists of LaBelle liked Roberts so much that they invited him to become the first fulltime pastor of their tiny wooden church, and he served for several years before returning to Wauchula.

In those days, Roberts staged baptisms whenever the spirit moved and the river water was warm enough. Today mass baptizings are becoming rare. For one thing, most rivers aren't clean enough. And today's churches have baptisteries inside where the ritual can be performed any time of year.

A 1920 revival meeting at LaBelle. *(Glenn Dyess, Florida Photographic Archives)*

42

PART TWO

The Way We Worked

A Store With Everything

Jehu J. Blount's General Store had it all. You could buy everything from live turtles to a casket. And if you needed a place to plant the casket, well, Blount had that, too.

J.J. Blount was one of Fort Myers' first merchants. He opened his store in the mid-1870s and proceeded to build up his stock to impressive proportions.

In pioneer days, a general store had to stock just about anything that might be needed in Florida's frontier communities: meat, fruits, vegetables, sugar, salt, cooking oil, flour, starch, whiskey; a wide range of dry goods, hats, coats, shirts, trousers, dresses, underwear, shoes and socks, sheets and blankets; saddles; guns and ammunition, and all manner of medicines.

Blount not only sold goods. He also bought and traded. From plume and alligator hunters, he bought plumes and hides and resold them to New York dealers.

An item from the *Fort Myers Press* of December 13, 1888: "Messrs. J.J. Blount & Co. shipped 280 white plumes last Friday. This is the first shipment of the season." And on June 13, 1889: "Blount & Co. have 13,000 gator hides ready for shipment.

Competition was tough in those days. Blount's store was on the northwest corner of First and Hendry Streets. On the northeast corner sat the store operated by W.M. Hendry, better known as Uncle Marion. Blount had married into the Hendry family, one of the most important in southwest Florida.

Jehu served the town as its official postmaster, without pay, until 1876 when the town acquired an official postmaster, Uncle Marion, with pay.

Blount began pulling strings. When Hendry's term expired, he was succeeded as postmaster by Howell Parker, Blount's partner. That brought the post office officially into Blount's store where Jehu figured it belonged.

Jehu Blount was born in north Florida. He served in the Third Seminole War and then fought with the Confederates in the Civil War, in a regiment commanded by Capt. F.A. Hendry. He married Hendry's sister then entered into the cattle business with his old C.O.

Later, he and Hendry dug the first drainage ditch in South Florida, Three Mile Canal, between Fort Thompson and Lake Okeechobee.

Not all his ventures were successful. The Panic of 1893 bankrupted a company he and others had formed to mine phosphate at a site near the Caloosahatchee River.

But, whether winning or losing, Jehu Blount remained one of Florida's most tireless pioneers. In addition to his cemetery, store, and cattle businesses he owned an orange grove, served on Fort Myers' first city commission and helped found the local First Methodist Church. He died in 1921 at the age of 82.

J.J. Blount's in 1886, note turtle on a leash in center foreground. *(Fort Myers Historical Museum)*

44

The Death of a Barefoot Mailman

Over one hundred years ago, a letter from Palm Beach to Miami was sent first to the lighthouse community at Jupiter. From there the letter went by Indian River steamer to the railhead at Titusville. Carried by train to New York, it was then sent by steamer to Havana. A trading schooner ferried it to Miami.

To reach a settlement only 68 miles away, a letter had to travel 3,000 miles. Elapsed time: as much as two months. You literally could have walked it there faster.

So, in 1885, the U.S. Post Office established a "barefoot route" and E.R. Bradley, of Lantana, was awarded the first mail-carrier's contract.

Bradley was paid $600 a year for making one trip a week between Hypoluxo, south of Lantana, and Miami. It took three days, one way, on foot and by boat.

The route stretched down the beach to the Hillsboro Inlet, where a rowboat was concealed. After crossing by boat, the mailman would then continue walking along the sands to the New River Inlet, which he also crossed by rowboat. From there he walked to Baker's Haulover (present-day Haulover Beach) at the head of Biscayne Bay, and then sailed 12 miles to the Miami Post Office.

Besides spending one night in Miami, the mailman also slept two nights each in the Fort Lauderdale and Orange Grove (Delray Beach) Houses of Refuge on the beach. Altogether, the route covered 136 miles, 56 via sailboat or rowboat and 80 miles on foot. The route lasted until 1892.

The mailman, carrying a specially-designed lightweight canvas mail pouch, walked barefoot along the water's edge where the sand was hard-packed.

After two years, Bradley had had enough of the physically demanding job. It was taken over with tragic consequences by George Charter and Ed Hamilton, a young Kentuckian who had moved to Hypoluxo Island.

The stormy fall of 1887 was not an easy time for barefoot travel. On Sunday, October 9, the lanky Hamilton, who was not feeling well, set out for Miami with the mail and a bottle of Perry Davis Pain-killer. He reached the Orange Grove House of Refuge without incident. He should have reached the Hillsboro Inlet by noon Monday, and he was due back in Hypoluxo on Saturday.

When he failed to return, George Charter set out to look for him. At the Hillsboro Inlet, he found Hamilton's clothing and knapsack containing the mail and the bottle of Perry Davis Pain-killer hanging from a sea grape tree.

But there was no trace of Hamilton. He was never seen again, and the service was halted five years later.

Apparently, someone had borrowed Hamilton's boat. Thus, it was not where it should have been, on the north side of the inlet, when he arrived. One theory states that he removed his clothes and attempted to swim across the inlet at a time when many alligators had been washed down to the area by the autumn storms.

What killed him? Alligators, sharks, or possibly the current was just too strong for a tough man who was not feeling his best.

Today, Ed Hamilton, the barefoot mailman, is honored by a plaque on the grounds of the Hillsboro Lighthouse.

Barefoot mailman Ed Hamilton, third from right. (*Historical Society of Palm Beach County*)

Key West Spongers Built an Empire

Look in my trunk and see what's there, sponger money,
One hundred dollars was my share, sponger money,
Sponger money never done, sponger money...

— Old Conch folk song

Not so long ago, Key West was the sponging capitol of the world. In 1895, some 1400 men and 300 boats were busy harvesting sponges from the floor of the shallow seas off the island city. It all added up to sponger money, money that was badly needed in a town that had seen two of its major sources of income – wreck salvaging and cigar-making – come and go.

Like the wreckers and the cigarmakers before them, Key West's spongers would enjoy only a brief moment of glory. But while it lasted, sponger money meant a hot time in town when the sponging boats came back to the docks at the foot of Elizabeth Street.

The sponge market started in 1849, when a New York freighter picked up a load of Key West sponges, at that time generally thought to be of little value. When the captain found a ready market for them, he returned and told the Conchs he would take all the quality sponges they could gather.

A sponge explosion followed. Within a few years, Key West was supplying 90 percent of all the sponges bought by Americans for industrial, hospital and home use.

The Conch approach to sponge-harvesting was primitive but effective. Two men worked from a small boat, one rowing, the other spotting the sponges through a glass-bottomed bucket and then gathering them with a long three-pronged pole. Bigger operations involved a schooner, towing eight to ten dinghies. The schooner might stay out as long as three months – however long it took to fill the boats with sponges.

Key West knew when the sponging boats were coming back. The smell of sponges drying ran miles ahead of them. No one liked the smell, but everyone liked sponger money.

In 1904, Greek colonists broke Key West's sponge monopoly by introducing hard-hat sponge diving from a base in Tarpon Springs. The Conchs did not give up without a fight. They burned two of the invading Greeks' boats, slashed air hoses and smashed equipment. But theirs was a losing battle. Wasteful methods of sponge harvesting over the years had depleted the Keys' beds, and the Conchs' primitive approach to sponging did not permit them to compete with the hard-hat divers farther afield.

Today, in Tarpon Springs, synthetic substitutes have turned the former Sponge Exchange into a shopping mall. And, in Key West, a handful of spongers still gather a small harvest, sold locally to the tourists. "Sponger money never done" is a phrase that now simple echoes a part of the Conch capitol's colorful past.

Sponges and spongers at Key West docks, ca. 1900. *(Historical Association of Southern Florida*

Clam Diggers of Marco Island

Not so long ago, Florida was short on ways to make a living. You could farm, hunt and fish. And if you lived on Marco Island you had one added opportunity – clams.

It was hard work, particularly around the turn of the century. But in its heyday, the clam industry provided jobs for some 200 people on the island.

Clam diggers stalked their quarry in knee-deep water, feeling for the mollusks with their bare feet and hoping they didn't happen upon a stingray. Boats from the canneries cruised by and bought the catch at 25 cents a bushel. On a good day a digger might harvest 30 bushels worth $7.50.

Along Florida's southwest coast lay some of the largest clam beds in the United States, covering about 150 miles of sea bottom. One, below Marco, was said to be 20 miles long and loaded with clams as large as a man's two fists.

However, Capt. Bill Collier, the biggest landowner on the island, had concluded that digging clams by hand wasn't efficient because the digging had to be limited to shallow water, low tides and calm seas.

In 1908, Capt. Bill invented a clam-dredging machine that worked so well it put most of the individual diggers out of business. The dredge brought up clams from as deep as 12 feet. With a crew of 25, it could gather 500 bushels of clams in a 12-hour shift.

With the dramatic increase in clams came the need for a new cannery. Collier brought J.H. Doxsee, whose family had been canning clams in Islip, Long Island, since 1867, to Marco to set up a cannery.

The Doxsees operated from 1910 to 1947. When the clam beds became "fished out" and the cannery closed, Marco plunged into deep depression until the 1960s. Then the island was parceled into plush real estate developments which promised their buyers "island living." But it was hardly the kind of island living those early clam diggers knew.

Clamboat on its way to cannery in Marco. *(Collier County Historical Museum)*

47

When Dania Was "Tomato Center of the World"

Nothing remains on the location of the old Dania railroad station. It sat for nearly seven decades on the east side of the tracks, just west of the present day Dania police station.

At the turn of the century, however, the depot was a busy place indeed for the passengers who rode Henry Flagler's Florida East Coast Railway and, even more important, for tomato farmers who needed to ship their produce to northern markets.

When Flagler pushed his railroad past Fort Lauderdale on its way to Miami in 1896, he opened up a whole new area for colonization, as it was then called. Today it would be called development.

Two new farming colonies were established south of Fort Lauderdale – Hallandale, a settlement of Swedes, and Modello, a community of Danes.

Modello was named for the Model Land Company, one of many businesses launched by Flagler, a great 19th-century tycoon. It was not a particularly good name to give a struggling young town, and fortunately the name was dropped after the Flagler people called another community in Dade County Modello.

The town's new name was Dania, in honor of its Danish population

Early settlers grew tomatoes. Each farmer packed his own produce and shipped it north on the railroad. In time, Dania would boast of two canning factories and 14 packing houses and lay claim to the title "Tomato Center of the World."

But all was not rosy for the early tomato "colonists." Since most of them came from the upper Midwest, they were hardly prepared for the heat of a Florida summer. Here they also faced mosquitoes, snakes, a scarcity of food in the early days and drinking water that was often contaminated by typhoid fever germs.

Still, by 1904 the colony was solidly on its feet. The time had come to convert a farming community into a town. On November 30, 1904, 28 of the town's 35 registered freeholders signed a charter calling for the incorporation of a town to be called Dania. It was the first incorporated town in what is now Broward County.

The old train station, built shortly after the railroad passed through, stood until the mid-1960s. Made of Dade County pine, it was the oldest building in Dania.

"They had to tear it down," recalls attorney Frank Adler, a long-time Dania resident. "It was damaged by Hurricane Cleo."

From the old station Adler has saved a few mementos – the brick pillars the station stood on and the sign that told passengers the train had arrived in Dania. And this is all that remains of what was, in its heyday, the only whistle stop between Palm Beach and Miami.

Crates of tomatoes at Dania depot. *(Broward County Historical Society)*

Working on the Overseas Railroad

Nobody ever said building a railroad from Homestead to Key West would be easy. It would have to reach more than a hundred miles into the Atlantic, connect scores of tiny islands, bridge deep, swift-flowing channels, and withstand the force of hurricanes.

Henry M. Flagler, owner of the Florida East Coast Railway, called it the toughest job he ever undertook. For the men who did the brutal manual labor, it was even tougher.

Construction began in 1905. The men had to battle heat, sand flies, rattlesnakes, alligators, crocodiles, and worst of all, mosquitoes. In October 1906, a hurricane claimed the lives of at least 130 men. By the time the job was finished, the death toll was in the hundreds.

Construction camps were built all along the Keys. Camp 10 was on Key Vaca, which became the project's headquarters. "Building this railroad has become a regular marathon," one worker remarked. Henceforth Camp 10 was known as Marathon – today the second-largest city in the Keys.

Flagler drew his work force from as far away as Spain and Italy, many laborers were blacks from the Caribbean. But the bulk came from good, solid American stock: to wit, winos from the skid rows of New York and Philadelphia. The pay: $1.25 a day.

One of the biggest problems was keeping the winos sober. Flagler banned liquor in the work camps but enterprising Key Westers maneuvered around the ban with "Booze Boats." Strait-laced residents countered with "Preacher Boats," sent to hold religious services.

Finally, after seven years, the 156-mile railroad reached Key West, on January 22, 1912. It had taken the labor of 20,000 men, and cost $50 million – more than half a billion in present-day dollars.

Payday for Keys railroad workers, 1906. *(Florida Photographic Archives)*

Dredging Up a Piece of History

The stout-hearted crew of the dipper-dredge *The Everglades* should have known they were in for trouble when they started work on a holiday, July 4, 1906.

It certainly turned out to be anything but a holiday for the crew of 18, captained by Henry Clay Cassidey, whose handlebar mustache bespoke authority. A second dredge, the *Okeechobee*, started operations on April Fool's Day, 1907. It figured.

Captain Cassidey and his crew faced a difficult task: to dig a canal from the south fork of the New River west through the Everglades and north toward Lake Okeechobee. It was the first cut through the wilderness to fulfill Florida Gov. Napoleon Bonaparte Broward's campaign promise to drain the Everglades.

Reed Bryan had been hired to supervise the construction of *The Everglades* and the *Okeechobee*. Working with machinery the state had purchased from a Chicago firm, Bryan set about building the dredges just across the river from where he, his brother Tom, and his father P.N. Bryan, were building the Bryan Hotel, later renamed the New River Inn and now the Discovery Center.

By April, 1906, Bryan had *The Everglades* ready to go. Gov. Broward came down from Tallahassee for the christening of the first of the two dredges. Reed's sister Constance smashed a bottle of champagne across the bow, and the face of South Florida was permanently changed.

Some time later, another dredge was to start south from the big lake, and with a little luck there was always the chance they might make connections and wind up with a 75-mile-long canal connecting Fort Lauderdale with Lake Okeechobee.

But luck does not always come to those in a hurry, and Broward's survey team was in a hurry, often surveying just ahead of the dredges, hammering in stakes for the giant machines to follow.

Mosquitos, snakes and the heat of the summer wore on the dredgers. By the end of 1907 the two dredges, which had been built at Sailboat Bend near present-day Third Avenue on the New River, had managed to dig only four and one-half miles of canal and reclaimed only about 12,000 acres. One of the project's doubters charged that at that rate it would take a century to reclaim a million acres.

Three years after *The Everglades* set out from Fort Lauderdale, another dredge, *Caloosahatchee*, started south from the lake. After about six miles the chief engineer surveyed a curve, instructed the crew to begin work the next day at a certain compass reading, then left for Fort Myers. The next morning the compass acted erratically, perhaps because of a severe electrical storm. At any rate, a six-mile error occurred.

Patching up the problem was difficult. Later, in trying to make connections with the dredge from the south, three men in two canoes set out to find *The Everglades*. The trio had to be rescued by the Fort Lauderdale crew, who found them exhausted, bitten up by mosquitos and weak from lack of food.

Somehow, in April of 1912, the job was completed. But the unruly compass left its legacy – a jog in the canal near the eastern entrance to Alligator Alley.

Broward, who came here often to visit Reed's project, is remembered in a different way. In 1915, when a new county was created out of parts of Dade and Palm Beach counties, it was named after the governor who dug ditches through South Florida, creating fortunes and controversy in the wake of the slow dredges.

The Everglades, 1906, Captain Cassidey at left. *(Fort Lauderdale Historical Society)*

When Boca Was a Suburb of Japan

Yamato Road stretches east across southern Palm Beach County, past the low-profile IBM plants to Federal Highway. At that intersection sits Boca Raton's Pylon Plaza, a wide range of successful businesses whose owners pride themselves on the architectural distinctiveness of the 5400 block of North Federal Highway.

But 80 odd years ago, the architecture was less distinctive and the population was less numerous, for the only business being done was farming and the people doing it were Japanese immigrants.

They called their settlement Yamato, an ancient name for Japan itself, pronounced with the accent on the first syllable, YA-ma-to. Virtually nothing remains of the colony they formed, but the word lingers on as an alternate name for Boca's 51st Street.

The colony was organized by Joseph Sakai, an idealistic young graduate of New York University, who saw farming colonies as a way of providing economic opportunity for his fellow countrymen. He was encouraged by the state and federal governments, as well as by Henry Flagler, the Palm Beach millionare who owned the Florida East Coast Railway, and who helped start other ethnic colonies including Dania which was first settled by Danes. Flagler contracted to supply the Yamato colony with its basic needs during its start-up near the community that was then known as Boca Ratone. (The lovely name, as we all know, translates to "mouth of the rat.")

Five colonists, admitted as students, arrived in the winter of 1904. As soon as they began to earn income from their principal crop of pineapples, they bought land and began constructing buildings.

The Japanese celebrated New Year's Day in 1905 with a party at which they entertained their American guests with songs and an exhibition of judo, tumbling and Japanese wrestling.

Heat, mosquitoes, flies and frequent flooding conspired to make life arduous for the colonists, who switched their cash crop to tomatoes after Cuban competition rendered pineapples unprofitable.

Despite their troubles, the colonists continued to acquire land and at one time their holdings reached as far east as the Intracoastal Waterway and as far west as Florida Atlantic University. The bulk of the Yamato settlement was along today's 51st Street near the railroad. Many of the buildings were near today's Boca Teeca subdivision.

Yamato school children with teacher Hildreth Gray, 1918.
(Boca Raton Historical Society)

Painting the Town Red

Early in this century, nearly everyone in Delray Beach grew pineapples. They were tasty in their own right, and what the settlers couldn't eat, they could sell.

Henry Flagler's pioneering railroad gave the homesteaders a means of shipping their produce north and earning a profit at a time when cash was in short supply throughout most of South Florida.

But later, the railroad created a problem for the growers. When Flagler extended his line to Key West in 1912, he opened up the pineapple business to more competition — too much competition as it turned out. Growers in Cuba shipped their pineapples to Key West and then on to the northeast by rail to sell at lower prices. Delray pineapple was no longer king.

Forced to look for another cash crop, Delray's growers switched to the ever-popular tomato. Soon, nearly everyone was growing tomatoes, in backyards or on whatever land was cleared.

The two biggest packers and shippers of tomatoes were Sundy's Feed and Fertilizer, and Chase & Co., both located along the railroad tracks in Delray.

Boys were employed by the pickers to make crates.

The girls packed tomatoes. Some could pack a hundred boxes a day. At five cents a box, that meant roughly $5 a day — about the same earnings as male crate-makers.

By 1916, the Snider Ketchup Company had entered the picture, buying the town's pineapple canning factory. Snider converted it to a ketchup cannery and became one of Delray's biggest employers.

"When quitting time came and the workers poured out into the street," wrote local historians Cecil and Margoann Farrar, "it looked like the whole town had spent the day making ketchup."

According to the Farrars, Snider's ketchup works brought one particularly significant change to Delray. The air, for many years sweet with the fragrance of pineapples, now became pungent with the smell of the crushed tomatoes, vinegar and spices used in making the red stuff.

It was an odd beginning for a town which has since become one of the Gold Coast's most attractive resort areas.

A load of Chase & Company tomatoes, ca. 1917. *(Delray Beach Historical Society)*

The Traveling Salesman Who Came to Stay in Delray

Delray Beach began as a settlement of 100 pioneers who arrived in 1895 from Michigan. The town was named Delray by an ex-railway mail clerk named Warren Blackmer, who hailed from a town of the same name.

Over the years, the settlers weathered freezes and crop failures, boom and bust. Today, the evidence of their final victory over hard times can be seen on the town's bustling east-west thoroughfare, Atlantic Avenue.

Atlantic has been a busy street for many years. But it was still a forgotten backwater when an Englishman named W.J. Cathcart built a two-story building there in 1912. The town had been incorporated only a year earlier, and the decision was made by just 26 registered voters.

Cathcart had discovered Florida's Atlantic coast as a traveling salesman who peddled notions – needles, pins, shoelaces and bolts of cloth. He drove a one-horse buggy up and down the coast between Jacksonville and Miami, struggling along a narrow road "paved" with glistening white oyster shells.

Around 1908, he decided he had knocked on enough doors. It was time to settle down. Delray was the place he chose.

Cathcart bought a general store owned by an eminent Lantana merchant, L.B. Lyman. Then, in 1912, he built a store of his own two blocks farther east on the northwest corner of Atlantic and Second Avenue. His business occupied the first floor.

The second floor of the Cathcart Building housed the offices of Dr. J.R. Cason, Jr., the town's first doctor, and Dr. William C. Williams, Dr. Cason, who came to Delray in 1905, drove the town's first car, a "one-lung" Reo.

Just to the east of the Cathcart Building was T.M. O'Neal's garage. O'Neal had come to Florida from Fairfax, South Carolina, in 1909 to work on the extension of Henry Flagler's railroad to Key West. He settled in Delray Beach, where he started a garage, later converting it into the town's first Ford dealership. Never far from the wonderful world of transportation, O'Neal also took care of horse-drawn travelers with a blacksmith's shop behind his garage.

Next to O'Neal's place was Harvel's meat market, operated by Roy Harvel, who would become the town's first Standard Oil distributor as more people purchased cars.

Cathcart's building must have been well constructed. Even though part of the back was blown off by the 1928 hurricane, it is still in use today – as Sal's Sport Shop.

The Cathcart Building on Atlantic Avenue, ca. 1914.
(Delray Beach Historical Society)

Raising Cane in Florida

Floridians have been raising cane for years. Columbus brought sugar cane to the New World in 1493, and Pedro Menendez introduced the sweet stuff to Florida in 1565, soon after he founded St. Augustine.

Since those early days, Florida has become the nation's number one grower of sugar cane, producing over a million tons a year of raw sugar.

But it hasn't been easy for either the growers or the harvesters. Sugar cane can't withstand severe cold or drought and is subject to a variety of plant diseases.

And when it comes to cutting it, the work is so hard that growers find themselves relying heavily on imported cane-cutters from the Caribbean. In an average seven-hour day a good Jamaican cane-cutter can chop 10 tons of cane. Cutters spend most of the day with their bodies bent at a 90-degree angle, which is why the work is usually described as back-breaking. A top cutter can earn nine dollars an hour.

Ruins of old cane mills and syrup vats can be found at various places around the state, most notably in the New Smyrna Beach area. There, efforts to raise sugar date all the way back to the 18th century, when the British ruled Florida.

In more recent times, many attempts were made to start sugar plantations and most of them ended in disaster. In 1884, for instance, Hamilton Disston launched his St. Cloud Sugar Plantation and his Sugar Belt Railroad on a site not far from today's Disney World. Disston had great dreams of reshaping South Florida to his liking by draining it. His dreams failed him, he killed himself and his sugar venture died, too.

John C. Grammling was a Miami judge who once successfully prosecuted John Ashley, South Florida's most celebrated outlaw, for murdering an Indian named DeSoto Tiger. The judge later tried his hand with sugar, forming the Moore Haven Sugar Corporation in 1920 on the west shore of Lake Okeechobee.

Like Disston, his dreams were big: 100 candy factories, 1,000 candy stores and a chain of restaurants where hungry eaters would spoon sugar onto cereal, strawberries and grapefruit and into coffee. But problems with machinery and flooding destroyed the company.

Miami itself once had a sugar mill. In 1924, the Pennsylvania Sugar Co. erected a mill on the Miami River 16 miles northwest of the city. Mining engineer Ernest Graham was sent to Dade County to run the company.

Pennsylvania Sugar failed, but Graham didn't. When the plant folded, he bought the company's land and raised vegetables, dairy cattle and the first governor from South Florida – Bob Graham, now a U.S. senator.

An important factor in Bob Graham's successful campaign in 1978 was his "workdays" program, in which he attempted to gain some insight into the world of a wide variety of working stiffs. Among countless other jobs, he worked on construction projects, on a movie set and as a salvage diver.

One "workday" he managed to avoid, however, was the most backbreaking job of all – chopping sugar cane.

Workers in cane field near Lake Okeechobee, ca. 1925.
(Historical Society of Palm Beach County)

All in the Family for Over 50 Years

As an immigrant from Russia near the turn of the century, Isadore Adler Sterling knew hard times. His family settled in Philadelphia, while he struck out as a dry goods peddler roaming the Southeast. Around 1930, he chose West Palm Beach as a base for his travels. A few years later, he settled down for good, opening a store in Fort Lauderdale on First Avenue near the New River.

Pop, as he was known, sold rugged work clothes to men struggling to keep food on the table during the Great Depression. Style was a luxury few could afford.

After serving with the Coast Guard in World War II, Pop's son, Morris, became a partner with his father. Together they shifted the store's inventory to designer clothes and sportswear of a more affluent time.

The Sterlings were among a handful of Jews in a town with an anti-Semitic reputation. But Pop had a way of breaking through ethnic barriers. His charity was legendary. He provided clothes for underpriviliged children, prisoners and disaster victims. He was known as a year-round "Jewish Santa Claus."

"I give back what has been given to me," Pop observed modestly. As for anti-Semitism, he said, "Doors were always opened to me."

A half-century later, so many doors opened that Pop's grandson, Neil Sterling, was elected a member of the Broward County School Board.

Pop died in 1979 at the age of 92. He outlived his son Morris, tragically slain in 1976 by a store employee suspected of embezzlement. At the time Neil Sterling was a pre-med student, as was his wife. When his father died, they left college and Neil took over the store.

M. Sterling, Broward County's oldest retail establishment, celebrated its golden anniversary in 1985. Nobody is certain exactly what day Pop opened his business in 1935, but that isn't important. His legacy endures.

Morris Sterling in his father's store, 1939. *(Fort Lauderdale Historical Society)*

Missionary in a Model-T

Nobody ever accused Harriet Bedell of standing still. As a missionary in Alaska, the Episcopal deaconess had covered the tractless waste on snowshoes and in dogsleds.

On Florida's Gulf Coast, as the missionary to the Seminoles, Bedell moved around the Big Cypress Swamp in a dugout canoe, on horseback and, later, in a second-hand Model-T Ford.

She became a familiar figure in her Model-T, cruising up and down the Tamiami Trail, visiting the Indian camps. She looked after the sick, helped the Seminole mothers care for their children, and encouraged the Indians to produce better handicrafts – decorated clothing, belts, wood carvings and other saleable items.

Bedell, who had no family of her own, came to Florida in 1932 to lecture on Alaska, where she had served the church as a missionary to the Indians for 16 years. She could take the cold; she came from Buffalo.

She didn't like what she saw in Miami. Curious tourists gawked at Indians on display at attractions. "Don't exhibit Indians, exhibit their crafts," she insisted.

Her church's Glade Cross Mission on the western edge of the Everglades had been inactive for 18 years. Time to get it started again, the deaconess decided. Bedell moved the mission site into Everglades City, then the seat of Collier County.

Twenty-seven years with the Indians had taught her patience. She preferred to bring the church's teachings to the Seminoles on a low-key, one-on-one basis. Seven years elapsed before she brought Indians together for a religious meeting.

Handicrafts provided a way to help the Seminoles rebuild their self-respect. She believed their arts and crafts were valuable, and proved it by selling them and returning the profits to the artisans.

Deaconess Bedell could be tough on them at times. She rejected any items that were not of the highest quality. She then placed the best of them in South Florida stores. Once a year, in the fall, she loaded up her old car and drove to New York to sell the handicrafts there. She made her solo drive to New York until she was in her 80s.

In 1960, Hurricane Donna swept through Collier County, wrecking the Glade Cross Mission. At 85, the deaconess finally agreed to move to the Bishop Crane Episcopal Home in Davenport, Fla. Even there she didn't really retire, preferring to continue speaking to groups, preparing Sunday School lessons and visiting the sick. Her explanation:

"There is no retirement in the service of the Master."

Deaconess Harriet Bedell with Seminoles in Collier County, 1940s. *(Fort Lauderdale Historical Society)*

Walking on Water in "Jesus Shoes"

Florida has been blessed with more than its share of inventors, one of whom discovered that even if you can't walk on water, it helps to have a machine that can.

Lamar Johnson was chief engineer for the Everglades Drainage District just after World War II. In 1946 Johnson faced a mammoth problem with water hyacinths. They had clogged up the freshwater canals and waterways throughout Southeast Florida.

Because hyacinths are not native plants, Florida's waters contain no natural checks and balances to slow them down. Consequently, they run wild, stopping boat traffic, uprooting wooden bridges and piers and killing fish. They even hamper poachers. Not to mention alligators. Manatees eat them, but not enough.

To fight the water weeds, Johnson needed a very specialized kind of wheel, outsized and capable of floating. These wheels were to be part of an amphibious contraption that could cruise across open water and then roll right up onto dense hyacinth mats and give them a dose of spray.

Unfortunately, the Everglades Drainage District had very limited funds, which was a familiar story. In 1931 it was forced to operate without any paid employees, just a volunteer board and a secretary.

In 1934 the district's West Palm Beach landlord served notice that EDD could remove no furniture or records from its office until it paid up its back rent – $1,140. Somehow, the district survived.

One day, Johnson saw a public utility line crew working along the highway. He noticed the huge reels that carried their supply of wire cable. He stopped and measured one of the reels, a good six feet high – just what he needed. Back at the office he did a few engineering calculations and found the reels would supply the flotation for the amphibious machine he hoped to put together. But when he tried to buy four of the reels from the utility, he found that the company's regulations forbade selling them to a state agency. The utility, however, had a solution.

"I was told that on a certain job four reels would be left behind when the crew moved out," Johnson later wrote in his book, *Beyond the Fourth Generation*. "If the reels turned up missing, the public utility company would not try too hard to find them. I took it from there."

Johnson next found a war surplus fourwheel-drive ammunition-carrier chassis in a Miami junkyard. EDD mechanics put together an ungainly vehicle by assembling the stripped-down chassis, a six-horsepower motor, a spray tank and the cable reels which were covered with thick marine plywood. At the back was a platform where a man could stand to spray hyacinths.

"It was a ridiculous-looking machine," Johnson admitted. But it worked. Launched on April 14, 1947, in southern Palm Beach County, it got the job done – until severe flooding that year led to the creation of a new, better-funded water management district.

Obviously, a contraption this weird had to have a name. Because it literally "walked on water," the workers irreverently dubbed it, "Jesus Shoes."

Custom-made aquatic weed destroyer. *(South Florida Water Management District)*

(South Florida Water Management District)

Woodsmen of the Big Cypress

The loggers, about 200 of them, set out each Monday morning, riding the train in shacks built on flatcars. Sometimes it took three hours to reach the big trees. The men played penny-ante poker on the 40-mile trip from Copeland into the Big Cypress Swamp.

Non-poker players watched the passing parade of wild-life: deer, otters, bears and panthers. They smiled when the train's wheels sliced up snakes sleeping on the tracks.

This was in the early 1950s, when the Lee Tidewater Cypress Co. was the world's largest cypress logger. Although smaller operators had been logging since the turn of the century, Tidewater owned two-thirds of the cypress timber in Collier County.

Its durability made southern bald cypress one of the most desirable of all woods. The problem was that it grew in the middle of swamps. Northern loggers could rely on rivers to move their wood to the sawmills, but Lee Tidewater had to build a railroad.

To fell the trees, loggers used a technique called gir-dling. They cut a complete circle into the trees' bark to kill them and drain them of water. Crew members earned about $70 a week. Among the job hazards were roving cottonmouth moccasins.

When work ended on Friday, the men rode the train back to Copeland, a company town built by Tidewater. Their families were waiting, and celebrated with trips to Janes General Store for food, drink and a blaring jukebox.

In its best year, Tidewater moved a third of a billion board feet from Collier County to its mill in Perry, north Florida. When the industry waned in the 1960s, the state began acquiring parcels of the cypress swamp.

Today Copeland is the site of a state prison, and the logging train no longer runs. But its roadbed is still there – used by hikers exploring the 15-mile Fakahatchee Strand trail.

Dragline rig in Big Cypress Swamp, ca. 1950. *(Collier County Historical Museum)*

PART THREE

The Way We Played

South Florida's First Regatta

Kirk Munroe, sportsman and popular author of boys' books, looked out across Biscayne Bay and noted with satisfaction the wide variety of sailboats anchored in front of almost every home in Coconut Grove.

He was particularly interested in *Ada*. It was, he wrote, "a boat of all work," but in earlier times had been the flagship of a New York yacht club. What, he wondered, would the old workhorse do in a race?

Ada belonged to Bill Brickell, who ran an Indian trading post at the mouth of the Miami River. He and his wife Mary were big landowners in South Florida.

As Washington's Birthday approached in 1887, Kirk concluded that the Bay now held enough boats for a regatta. With Ralph Munroe, a Coconut Grove boat designer, he set about lining up a race for the holiday, always a big occasion in Coconut Grove.

On February 15, 1887, four enthusiastic sailors met at Kirk's home to plan the area's first regatta. The home bore the strange name Scrububs, a word that amused Kirk some years earlier when it spilled from the mouth of a young boy trying to pronounce "suburbs."

Fifteen Biscayne Bay boats entered: six dinghies, com-prising a small boat class, six yachts under 35 feet which made up Second Class, and three boats 35 and over, the First Class sailboats.

Ada, with Brickell at the helm, sailed in the big boat class, competing with two large sharpies, *Pelican,* owned by the Hine brothers from New Jersey, and *Amy,* owned by Frederick S. Morse, a direct descendant of Samuel Morse, progenitor of one of America's most famous families.

Winners were the hard-working *Ada* in 35 and over and Dick Carney's *Maggie* in 35 and under. The small boat winner was *Edna,* owned by an old Indian scout, John Addison. He lived in an area called the Hunting Grounds, known these days as Cutler.

From the enthusiasm spun off the regatta, Kirk and Ralph Munroe formed the Biscayne Bay Yacht Club, which celebrated it 100th anniversary in 1987. It is appropriate that the oldest organization on the south-east Florida mainland should be a boating club.

The first Biscayne Bay Yacht Club Regatta, 1887. *(Historical Association of Southern Florida)*

A Man Who Did Things First

Kirk Munroe was a busy man. When he wasn't writing one of his 35 books for boys, he was eagerly pursuing a lifelong enthusiasm for outdoor sports of all kinds.

He brought South Florida its first yacht racing club, its first tennis court and its first baseball team. Just so there wasn't any spare time wasted, he and his wife also started Coconut Grove's first library – with help from Mrs. Andrew Carnegie – and Munroe helped start the Florida Audubon Society and Miami's first Boy Scout troop.

Before coming to Florida, the Wisconsin-born writer lived in New York, where he became editor of *Harper's Young People* in 1879. While living in the big city, he founded the American Canoe Association and served as commodore of the New York Canoe Club. Munroe then induced members of the club to try their luck with a new-fangled contraption called a bicycle. He went on to organize the New York Bicycle Club and later the League of American Wheelmen, with a membership at the time of more than 100,000.

In 1883 he married Scottish-born Mary Barr, daughter of novelist Amelia Barr. On their honeymoon Kirk and Mary canoed down the St. John's River and decided to call Florida home.

They settled first on Lake Worth, then moved on to a Biscayne Bay community called Cocoanut Grove, later changed to Coconut Grove at the insistence of Mary.

Kirk concluded in 1887 that there were enough boats on the bay to hold a regatta. He and a neighbor proceeded to form the nation's southernmost boating club, the Biscayne Bay Yacht Club.

Mary Munroe kept a diary and despite her baffling handwriting, it is possible to decipher an occasional entry, like the following:

"February 12, 1892 – I had a game of tennis, the first here and my first game – Kirk's tennis court is the first here and the game this afternoon was the first played."

"June 4, 1892 – Kirk attended a baseball meeting this morning. The club will be called the Coconut Grove Base Ball Club. He came home quite excited about it all."

It is difficult today to appreciate how popular Kirk Munroe's books were, but in 1893 the Knights and Ladies of the Round Table, a nationwide organization of 200,000 children, assembled at the Chicago World's Fair to greet their favorite authors. Voted most popular was Kirk himself.

Kirk Munroe with two Coconut Grove lads, ca. 1890.
(Ralph Munroe, Historical Association of Southern Florida)

Sailing Back Home to Miami

The old sailboat is pushing a hundred now. She's not in the water anymore, sitting instead inside a covered shed. But at least she's home again.

Micco, a 50-foot sailboat, was designed by Commodore Ralph Munroe, of Coconut Grove, and built for him at Tottenville, New York, in 1891. It was a big year for the commodore; he also designed and built his South Florida home, the Barnacle.

Micco proved highly seaworthy, making the run from Cape Canaveral to Jupiter, a distance of 105 nautical miles, in ten hours before a fierce northerly wind.

The following year, the commodore piloted her north from Cape Florida to Sandy Hook, New York, in six-and-a-half days. *Micco's* record for boats in her class stood for years.

A year after she was built, Munroe sold her to Arthur Merriman, of Manchester, Massachusetts. Munroe hated to see her go, but he was a designer who created boats, sold them, then moved on to new designs.

Away from Florida's waters, *Micco* continued to make a name for herself. At age 33, in 1924 she joined the Atlantic Yacht Club fleet cruise, finishing second in a fleet of all sizes. That same year she came in second in her class in the prestigious Bermuda Race.

A half-century later, the State of Florida bought Munroe's home – and that same year the *Micco* was unexpectedly heard from again. A young Woods Hole, Massachusetts, marine biologist wrote that he was leaving the country and would like to sell Florida the boat on which he was living – none other than the venerable *Micco*.

Today, a visit to Barnacle State Park in Miami provides a tour of Commodore Munroe's colorful old house – and a look at a traveling sailboat that left Miami for New England, then made her way back home 80 years later.

Micco under sail, 1891. *(Ralph Munroe, Historical Association of Southern Florida)*

To Jupiter, in Search of Wild Game

It was in the 1880s that big-game hunters first "discovered" Jupiter.

Around that time, wealthy visitors from the North were beginning to enjoy the winter wonders of a nearby settlement which in 1886 would officially take the name Palm Beach. Most of them came down in yachts for cruising and fishing. But what else was there to do?

They soon found out. Year-round residents had long ago learned that hunting was excellent in the area. To them it was a means of staying alive. The winter visitors took it up to survive the boredom.

One particularly good hunting spot was Jupiter, where the red lighthouse towered above the confluence of the Indian and Loxahatchee Rivers. From Palm Beach, hunters could cruise north some 10 miles, sail through the Jupiter Inlet and find themselves in a land which abounded in rabbits, squirrels, ducks and quail, and more sizable game including wild turkey, deer, panther and bear.

Deer were plentiful along Florida's southeast coast, but a hunter had to work to kill a panther or bear. The big cats, scarce even then, had to be tracked, usually by an experienced guide who knew the territory. Bears were taken at night when they came down to the inlets to hunt for sea turtles and turtle eggs. Moonlit nights were the best time to "sit for bear."

Two winter visitors who especially enjoyed the hunting at Jupiter were Tom Carnegie and Commodore Charles J. Clarke. Both men were from Pittsburgh.

A native of Scotland, Tom was the younger brother of Andrew Carnegie and a partner with Andrew in an iron and steel venture which was enjoying considerable success. In time, it became known as U.S. Steel.

Commodore Clarke, a shipping magnate, built one of Palm Beach's earliest mansions, named Primavera. Some called it the Spanish House because of its tile roof. Clarke kept a crew of 12 at Primavera to manage his boats and docks – which left plenty of time for hunting.

Despite its discovery by hunters, Jupiter remained an out-of-the-way city until the 1960s, when upstart neighbor Tequesta began to outstrip the older, sleepy town. Famous citizens have included singer Perry Como and actor Burt Reynolds.

Tom Carnegie, cradling rifle, and Commodore Charles Clarke on the stern of their hunting boat at Jupiter, ca. 1885.
(Historical Society of Palm Beach County)

The Original Panther Man

At one time, a man could pose with pride over a panther he had killed. Now it is a shameful act, a felony punishable by fine and imprisonment. Times change.

Charles Cory inherited money from his father's wine and silk business and he knew how to enjoy it. His opulent houseboat *Wanderer,* anchored in the New River in the 1890s, was Fort Lauderdale's first luxury housing.

The gun room on his houseboat contained one of the most elaborate collections of firearms to be found anywhere in this country. "There were enough weapons," said one oldtimer, "to have re-opened the Seminole War at a moment's notice."

Fighting Seminoles, however, was not Cory's style. He spent a great deal of time studying their culture and language. In his book *Hunting and Fishing In Florida,* he compiled one of the most complete Seminole vocabularies ever assembled.

But when he had gun in hand, Cory was more inclined to stalk the game that abounded in the woods nearby. His hunting safaris were joyful extravaganzas, played out on a grand scale.

A Cory panther hunt to Hillsboro River would involve a team of mighty hunters on horseback, Seminole guides, usually led by an astute Indian named Charlie Willie,

Cory's chef, and a wagon filled with supplies that included the latest and best in tents and cots. It would never do for a Cory guest to sleep on the ground. His guest list included then-President Grover Cleveland, Admiral George Dewey, and actor Joseph Jefferson.

For Cory, the hunt was a great lark to be stretched out and savored, until the party grew tired of the chase, usually after about 10 days. Most of the time, Charlie Willie could have scared up a panther the first day out. But he knew better.

Today, the Florida panther is a critically endangered species; fewer than 100 are thought to exist. But Cory should be judged by the laws of his time, and perhaps, by his words:

"Many a flock of quails or ducks I have watched feeding without disturbing them," he wrote, "and many a deer I have stalked, and perhaps photographed and then watched from my concealment until, discovering my presence, it bounded away unharmed. It should be a rule with every true sportsman never to kill more game than can be properly used."

Charles Cory with a trophy panther. *(Fort Lauderdale Historical Society)*

66

When Casinos Were for Bathers

When you drive along Fort Lauderdale beach, even in winter, you see so many scantily-clad sun worshippers that it is hard to imagine a time when the sands were nearly deserted.

But there was such a time. In the early days of the 20th century, there was no ready transportation from the populated areas near New River over to the blue waters of the Atlantic. You could make it if you had your own boat, but even then you had to contend with a walk to the beach over marshy terrain, as mosquitoes swarmed around your sweaty brow. Or, you could swim the Intracoastal Waterway, but that was so shallow you would have to wade part way, an invitation for stingrays to slash your legs with barbs.

By 1915, enough people were venturing across to the beach to justify the construction of a wooden municipal casino. The city-built casino was a two-story structure with a dance floor on the second story.

At first the casino was only open on Sundays, when excursion boats, such as Captain Dick La Vigne's *Excelsior*, made regular runs from the mainland over to the beach island. Once Las Olas Boulevard and Bridge were completed in 1917, the casino was open every day.

During the boom years of the 1920s, the beach became a popular hangout not only for the locals but also for tourists, who, for the first time, were becoming important to the city's economy. Even in the uninhibited Roaring Twenties, bathing attire remained modest by today's string bikini standards.

Lasting fame did not come to the local sands, however, until the publication of a book by Glendon Swarthout and the Joe Pasternak-produced movie of the same name, *Where the Boys Are*. Connie Francis sang the title song.

Three months after the movie's world premiere at the Gateway Theater on December 21, 1960, the beach was mobbed with college students – girls as well as boys – on spring break. That was the first of what became an annual rite of spring.

Fort Lauderdale Beach, 1925. *(Broward County Historical Commission)*

Racing Against the Wind

Fulford Speedway had its day of glory. Unfortunately, one day was all the fates allotted the auto racing track in north Dade County.

On that one glorious day, February 22, 1926, the stands were jammed with 20,000 fans as America's top auto racers, flagged on by the legendary Barney Oldfield, smashed distance records of 100 to 300 miles on an elevated wooden track.

Ahead lay many more great racing extravaganzas, or so Fulford's promoters thought. But it was not to be. Six months later, the infamous 1926 hurricane swept in and blew Fulford Speedway away.

Carl Fisher, developer of Miami Beach and the Indianapolis Speedway, started the Fulford Speedway in 1925. But before Fulford was built, finding a good track surface had been a problem. Horse racing tracks were too soft, dusty and flat. Brick tracks were too expensive. Asphalt tracks not durable enough.

So in 1910 a wooden track was built, in Playa del Rey, Calif. Using basic bridge construction techniques, the track was built from 2x8 boards laid over pilings. The track was the first of 24 to be constructed across the country during the next 21 years.

The wood usually began to deteriorate after three years. Holes would develop in the raised tracks during races and carpenters were kept busy repairing the damage while the races went on. Wilbur Shaw, racing along at 130 m.p.h., once saw a human head pop up in the middle of the track. It belonged to a carpenter standing underneath the track.

When Carl Fisher built his track in 1925, he chose Ray Harroun, winner of the first Indy 500, as its designer. The track featured turns banked at a lofty 50 degrees, 18 degrees higher than those at Daytona Beach.

Excitement built in Miami that February day in 1926 as the country's top drivers held trial runs. Eighteen cars – three Dusenbergs, 14 Millers and one Miller Front Wheel Drive – were entered, manned by such eminent racers as two-time Indy champion Tommy Milton and the 1925 Indy winner, Peter DePaulo, both driving Dusenbergs. All of the drivers received $1,500 in appearance money.

Fans paid $3 to stand in the infield, $6 to $8 to sit in the grandstands, $10 to $15 to camp in a ritzy box seat. Even the flags were different in those days. A red flag waved by Oldfield didn't mean "stop"; it meant the course was clear.

At 230 miles, DePaulo took the lead and held it the rest of the way. His winning average speed of 129.295, a world's record for 300 miles, earned him first prize of $12,000. He made the 300-mile trip without a pit stop.

Six months later, Fulford Speedway was history. The raceway was never rebuilt. Instead, a million feet of boards, salvaged from the storm, were used to rebuild the nearby town. Today, the town is known as North Miami Beach.

Fulford Speedway, 1926. *(Florida Photographic Archives)*

When the Ponies Ran (Illegally) at Pompano

Today, Pompano Park in southwest Pompano Beach enjoys the distinction of offering Florida sports fans the only track in the state where they can wager on harness racing. The track opened more than two decades ago and horses have trotted and paced merrily along ever since.

The first Pompano Race Track, on the same site, was less successful.

Built in 1926 at a cost of $1.25 million, the track was a mile long, 100 feet wide and surfaced with clay and sand. The grandstand provided seating for 6,800 spectators and stables and service buildings for 1,000 horses, early accounts claim.

Special buses brought thousands of fans to the track for its opening on Christmas Day, 1926. There was one serious problem, however. In those days parimutuel betting, vital to the prosperity of a track, was illegal. In the Roaring Twenties, the authorities often looked the other way. Not so with Pompano. Gov. John Martin called Pompano "a center of lawbreakers" and threatened to "send the militia down there with a tractor and plow up the Pompano track and plant it in cowpeas." The threat worked.

From the start, the Pompano track was doomed. Its owners used it for boxing matches and automobile racing, but nothing worked.

In 1928, a hurricane struck South Florida, killing nearly 2,000 people, most of them migrant workers near Lake Okeechobee. The Red Cross set up shelters at the Pompano Race Track to care for more than 1,000 storm victims.

In the 1940s, a Kentucky sportsman named Frederick Van Lennep spotted the remains of the old Pompano track as he flew over the area in an airplane. Later he purchased the property and constructed a totally new facility which opened on February 4, 1964 to a crowd of 6,559.

Recent years have seen quarter horse and Appaloosa racing added to the trotting menu at Pompano. On December 27, 1980, the track saw the farewell race of Niatross, one of harness racing's greatest pacers, before more than 18,000 racing fans.

Parking lot and administration building at first Pompano race track, 1926. (*Pompano Beach Public Library*)

When Kids Played in the Caves of Palm Beach

You don't really expect to find caves along the southeast Florida coast. Maybe that's why they were such good hiding places.

You can't crawl into them any more. The press of civilization has simply filled them in. The rocky outcroppings that serve as reminders of the caves lie now on private property, hidden away among sea grape trees in the posh Gold Coast town of Gulfstream.

Tom McGinty, of nearby Ocean Ridge, remembers the caves with Tom Sawyer-like affection. "You weren't supposed to play in them," he says. "You had to look out for rattlesnakes."

During the Civil War, there were no settlements near Gulfstream, or anywhere else in today's Palm Beach County. It was a lonely trip for Long John Holman, the first barefoot mailman, as he trudged along the beach, carrying the mail from Biscayne Bay to St. Augustine. Unlike later barefoot mailmen, who kept provisions and boats stashed along an abbreviated route, Holman's treks appear to have been an occasional service, and it took him several weeks to deliver a letter.

One of Long John's stopovers was a coral rock formation that housed caves where he could come in out of the rain or the sun or could hide from any hostile Indians that might be nearby.

The rock formation extended from the edge of the ocean through the ocean ridge and emerged to the west of the ridge, where the entrance to the caves lay. The larger cave was about 20 by 20 feet, high enough for a grown man to stand upright. A flat stone inside the cave could be used as a table. Local legend said that pirate treasure was hidden beneath the tablestone, but no one could ever move it to find out.

The second cave opened into the main cavern by a crawlway. Unfortunately, it was pitch black inside. No matter how hot it was outside, both caves stayed cool.

The caves even found their way into children's literature in W.J. "Pat" Enright's book, *Sailor Jim's Cave*.

Gilbert L. Voss, noted University of Miami oceanographer and author, remembers playing in the caves as a child.

"You had to bend down to walk into the big cave," he recalls. "To get to the second cave you had to crawl. You could still go into them in the 1970s."

Young Chuck Pierce, who would become the president of the First National Bank of Fort Lauderdale, at the entrance to the caves, ca. 1910. *(Mary Linehan)*

Playing Up a Storm in Sandspur Stadium

Sandspur Stadium. That's what football players at the University of Miami called the field where they played their first season. Bereft of grass, the "field" was just a layer of mulch spread over a base of coral rock.

But they were lucky to have that much.

When the University of Miami opened in 1926, plans were announed to build a temporary, 8,000-seat stadium on campus. Work started on September 15, 1926, just 48 hours before one of the deadliest hurricanes in history struck South Florida.

When the winds subsided, a makeshift grandstand was erected with lumber from a dismantled Coral Gables stadium. The season opened on October 23, and fans were enthusiastic. They just weren't numerous. Only 304 turned out to watch Miami beat Winter Park's Rollins College 7-0.

Miami's first coach was Howard "Cub" Buck, a two-time All-American from the University of Wisconsin. Considering that he only began organizing the team two weeks before classes started, his results were remarkable.

Playing a freshman schedule, UM was undefeated in eight games. This included two against the University of Havana; the first game was at Coral Gables on Thanksgiving Day, the second in Cuba on Christmas Day. Miami won both 23-0.

Center Bill Kimbrough was the team's captain, and later became the chief of police of Coral Gables. At fullback was Ted Bleier, whose nephew Rocky would later play for the Pittsburgh Steelers. The biggest player was a 190-pound tackle named Larry Catha. He enrolled at the university after working for the Florida East Coast Railway.

It was during the first season that the unnamed team found its moniker. One of the players, Porter Norris, came up with an obvious nickname – the Hurricanes. With memories painfully fresh of the death and destruction of the September storm, many found the name offensive.

But it stuck. Years later, to no avail, people were still blasting it, most notably the late billionare John D. MacArthur. "Why keep reminding people there are Florida hurricanes?" he asked.

But as recent storms have shown, it never hurts to remind Floridians of nature's destructive fury.

UM 22, Merccr 6, November 6, 1926 at Sandspur Stadium.
(Historical Association of Southern Florida)

He Shot an Arrow to the Stars

Remember the days when your friendly neighborhood movie theater showed short subjects along with the feature film?

Howard Hill produced and starred in many of these selected shorts, displaying his considerable skill with a bow and arrow. His motion picture production company specialized in producing outdoor documentaries.

One of his assignments was to train Errol Flynn for the archery sequences in the 1938 film *Robin Hood*.

Hill owed his successful movie career to Glenn H. Curtiss, aviation pioneer and developer of such South Florida 1920s boom towns as Hialeah, Miami Springs and Opa-locka.

Curtiss was an archery nut. He was particularly addicted to a sport called archery golf. In this hybrid, the player replaces the golf ball with an arrow and the No. 2 wood with a bow. Instead of putting the ball into the cup, he shoots an arrow through an iron ring – or, in Curtiss' version, into a coconut.

The aviator organized the Opa-locka Archery Golf Club and eagerly sought members. As an incentive to beginning archers, he fastened $20 gold pieces to trees. If you could hit them, you could keep them.

Curtiss needed a coach for his club. He found one in Howard Hill, a young Creek Indian who had just arrived in Miami from Alabama, where he had learned to hunt game with bow and arrow. Hill introduced Curtiss to bow hunting and soon the developer had another enthusiasm.

The two men organized bobcat hunts on the northeast shores of Lake Okeechobee and also traveled to the Okefenokee Swamp, in Georgia, to hunt bear with bow and arrow.

To return the favor, Curtiss introduced his friend to the camera. Soon Hill's knowledge of photography rivalled his grasp of archery.

After Glenn Curtiss died in 1930, Hill moved on to Hollywood, where he formed his own production company. He always gave full credit for his success to the man he called "G.H.," a man he later wrote of as "an archer, a gentleman and a true sportsman."

Howard Hill with youthful pupil, ca. 1930. (*Romer Collection, Miami-Dade Public Library*)

Big Hunt for a Little Deer

They called him "el aeroplano," a tiny Key deer so fast he seemed to fly. El aeroplano eluded hunters for 10 years before he was finally bagged on Big Torch Key, with the aid of a legendary deerhound named "Ha-Ha."

That was in the 1930s, when deer hunting flourished in the Keys. Most of the deer hunters were Cubans, former cigar-makers from Key West, who used "exploradores," the Spanish equivalent of hunting guides. It was one of the exploradores, a man named Tertulino, who caught the legendary el aeroplano.

Tertulino and Julio Pui were considered the island city's two most effective exploradores, each man serving his particular group of followers as "el capitan" of the hunt.

"I have hunted deer on the Keys for many, many years," Pui told author Stetson Kennedy, "and my father he hunt before me. Also, I have hunt deer in Cuba and the West Indies."

The Key deer is a sub-species, a smaller version of the Virginia white tail, less than three feet high at the shoulder. A buck averages 65 to 80 pounds, a doe about 40. Over many years the deer has adapted to the aquatic world of the Keys.

"They are very clean, have few ticks, and their flesh is of excellent flavor," said Pui. "And fast – they almost fly."

By the 1930s, hunting had depleted the number of Key deer to 20. In 1939 the Florida Legislature banned deer hunting in the Keys. Since then, the efforts of many conservationists and agencies have helped the tiny deer to make a comeback. The effort culminated in 1963 with the dedication of the National Key Deer Refuge.

Today, between 250 and 300 tiny deer roam the Florida Keys, mostly on Big Pine, Cudjoe and Sugarloaf Keys, protected within the roughly 5,000 acres managed by the National Key Deer Refuge.

Under the care of the U.S. Fish and Wildlife Service, the population once rose to a high of 400. But new dangers have again reduced their numbers. Development is shrinking their habitat, dogs are harassing them, and cars have taken their toll. More than 30 were killed by motorists on U.S. 1 during 1986.

But the Key deer survive, just as in the days of el aeroplano. And today, stalkers are more likely to be armed with curiosity and a camera than a gun. Says Charlie Case, assistant refuge manager: "The best way to see the deer is to drive out to Key Deer Boulevard on Big Pine late in the evening. That's when you'll see them."

Key deer hunter with hounds and trophies, late 1930s.
(Stetson Kennedy)

The Amazing Exploits of Little Katy

In these days of specialization, a worldclass swimmer doesn't dive and a diver doesn't swim. One or the other, take your choice.

But Katherine Rawls didn't favor specialization. She did things her way, which is to say she entered any event she wanted and won just about everything the world of swimming had to offer.

Little Katy, the pride of Fort Lauderdale High School, became the only aquatic star, male or female, ever to win national championships in swimming and diving.

Historian August Burghard, himself a swimmer of note, wrote: "It is difficult to imagine two sports – swimming and diving – so totally different. Few achieve total excellence in both. I have seen divers with only enough swimming ability to get out of the pool after a dive. Many swimmers would injure themselves if they attempted the more intricate dives. Yet Rawls mastered both fields and was a champion in each."

A tiny 5-foot-2, and 107 pounds, Katy first began to develop her swimming skills in the freshwater lakes of Central Florida, where her father was working in road construction. Later, the family moved to Hollywood, to Coral Gables and then to Fort Lauderdale.

During the 1930s, Katy Rawls competed in springboard and platform diving, and freestyle, medley and breaststroke swimming, winning 33 national titles and a string of U.S. and world records. Her greatest day came on September 3, 1934, the second day of a swimming decathlon celebrating the opening of New York's Jones Beach. Katy won all 10 women's events.

Only one prize eluded her – an Olympic Gold Medal. In 1932, at 14, she won a Bronze Medal at Los Angeles in springboard diving, and four years later in Hitler's Germany she earned another Bronze, this time in the freestyle medley relay.

By 1940, the Olympics had become one of the many casualties of World War II. Katy Rawls turned to another kind of competition.

As a friend of Tony Piper, son of the founder of Piper Aviation, she had become interested in flying. She eventually married her flight instructor, Ted Thompson. When war came, the U.S. Army Air Force needed qualified women fliers to ferry planes across the ocean to overseas war zones. Katy was one of 25 American women named to launch the Women's Air Force Service Pilots, better known as WASPS.

And, once again, Katy Rawls proved she could handle anything to do with water: swimming through it, diving into it – or flying over it.

Katy Rawls accepts congratulations at a 1935 Fort Lauderdale swimming meet. *(Fort Lauderdale Historical Society)*

Wynnes Dangerous Win

In the 1960s, racing powerboats through the pounding waters of the Gulf Stream was a demanding sport that left boaters with assorted bruises and broken bones and deposited many a costly experimental boat on the floor of the briny.

One of the weirdest of these colorful races took place on February 22, 1966. It was a miserable day, windy and rainy, but since it stopped somewhere short of a hurricane, the weather failed to deter 30 boats from setting out that morning from Miami's Dinner Key in the annual Sam Griffith Memorial Ocean Race. They would try to cover a grueling 172-mile run to Fort Lauderdale to Bimini to Cat Cay, then back to Miami.

A tense duel shaped up between two Miami boat builders, Dick Bertram and Jim Wynne. The bearded Wynne had won the World Offshore Powerboat Championship in 1964, only to lose it the following year to Bertram in his *Brave Moppie*.

To regain his title, Wynne needed a victory in the 1966 Griffith. He was entering the event with *Thunderbird*, a boat of his own design, powered by a revolutionary propulsion system, two ST6 Pratt & Whitney Aircraft gas turbines built by United Aircraft of Canada.

How rough was the weather that day? Within two hours of the start, 25 of the 30 entries had been forced out by breakdowns or by injuries to their crews. The most spectacular of the casualties was Bertram's world championship boat. *Brave Moppie* sank stern first in 90 fathoms.

Wynne crossed the finish line 70 miles ahead of his nearest competitor. Two and a half hours later, the only other boat to finish reached Miami. Jerry Langer, who made it in a 20-foot fiberglass outboard, was promptly declared winner of the $3,000 prize money.

Thunderbird's gas turbines were ruled too experimental. But the first-place finish counted for driver points, and clinched Wynne's second world's championship.

As tough as it was, that race must have seemed a cakewalk compared to an earlier boating feat. Back in 1958, Wynne and a Dane named Ole Botved had crossed the Atlantic from Copenhagen to New York in a 22-foot wooden powerboat driven by two 50-horsepower outboard motors. Asked if he would ever try it again, Wynne replied, "Hell, no."

Jim Wynne's experimental *Thunderbird*. (Jim Wynne)

A Trophy-Winning "Minnow"

There are few more recognizable or popular atheletes in the world today than Chris Evert. She has won more major tennis titles than any other player in the history of the game, male or female.

Yet there was a time when she was just a little girl growing up in Wilton Manors and later in Fort Lauderdale. Her nickname then was "The Minnow."

Chris' father, Jimmy Evert, the tennis pro at Fort Lauderdale's Holiday Park courts, had been a tough, competitive player. He was a national 18-and-under indoor champion in 1940, winner of a national title in Canada and captain of the University of Notre Dame tennis team.

"I liked to have my children near me when I worked," he said. "Chris grew up around a tennis court."

With five children, he was always assured of a mini-crowd at Holiday Park. Back in the 1960s, Chris was growing up surrounded by good tennis players. She soon emerged from the pack as a player of rare ability. By the time she was 12, Chris was state champion in her age group, and two years later was No. 1 nationally in the 14-and-under category.

In January 1969, when she was 14, she competed in the Austin Smith Tennis Championships held at Holiday Park. Her father, as host pro, was the tournament chairman.

Free-lance photographer Gene Hyde snapped a picture of her gazing wistfully at the winner's prize. That was as close as she got to it that year. The women's title was won by Stephanie De Fina of Hollywood, ranked ninth nationally.

Chris would eventually win the Austin Smith title, along with over 150 others, including Wimbledon and the U.S. Open.

Looking at Hyde's photograph more than 15 years later, Chris, a durable, battletoughened veteran of the international tennis wars, smiled and said, somewhat sadly, "Innocent, I was so innocent when I played that tournament."

Chris Evert, age 14, holds silver plate that eluded her.
(Gene Hyde, Fort Lauderdale Historical Society)

PART FOUR

Events, Cataclysmic and Mundane

The Spanish-American War and South Florida

Secretary of State John Hay called it "a splendid little war." Some would argue that his description of the Spanish-American War was not quite accurate. Especially for Floridians.

At Jupiter, a better word would have been terrifying; at Miami, nightmarish; at Key West, thirsty; and at Tampa, overwhelming. But decidedly not "splendid."

Try to picture the tiny town of Jupiter, population about 100, on May 24, 1898. Rumors had persisted for weeks that the Spanish fleet might come up from Cuba and try to shell the towns along the southeast Florida coast, maybe even come ashore to burn and pillage.

Then, just before sundown, a monster of a battleship steamed in closer and closer and dropped anchor just off the Jupiter shore. She carried no flags, no identification.

"What is your name?" signaled a nervous James Cronk, who ran both the signal station and the weather bureau at Jupiter Inlet. No answer.

"Where are you from?" he asked. Still, no answer.

Cronk was worried. After all, little Jupiter was an important communication link, boasting a lighthouse, a weather bureau, a signal station, and a telegraph station located where the cable from the West Indies terminated.

Uneasy men gathered their firearms and assembled on the south bank of the Loxahatchee River, near the telegraph station. Cronk, still watching from his signal tower, saw a boat being lowered. Armed men with lighted lanterns climbed aboard. The boat approached the coast, then headed through Jupiter's treacherous inlet.

The townsfolk braced, determined to fight to the finish. The boat came closer, close enough to see the sailor's faces and recognize their uniforms. They were U.S. sailors. Jupiter was relieved. And so was the U.S. Navy.

The monster ship offshore was the *USS Oregon*, declared by some to be the mightiest battleship in the world:

Troops muster near Miami's Royal Palm Hotel. *(Florida Photographic Archives)*

General Miles, seated second from right, and staff visiting General Wheeler, third from left, Tampa. *(Florida Photographic Archives)*

12,000 tons, nearly 500 men, heavy armor, big guns.

When she left San Francisco on March 19, bound for the North Atlantic, war with Spain was imminent. During the course of the *Oregon's* 16,000-mile, 66-day trip from San Francisco to Jupiter, the United States declared war on Spain.

To stay hidden from the Spanish fleet, the *Oregon* transmitted no signals that might reveal her location to the Spaniards, or, as it turned out, to the Americans either. To the Navy, her floating fortress was "lost."

It was a mighty big ship to "lose." But, then, it was that kind of war.

The commanding U.S. general weighed over 300 pounds, suffered from gout, had trouble moving about and had to sleep on a dismantled door. No beds were big enough for Gen. W.R. Shafter.

President William McKinley had tried to put some of the bitterness of the Civil War behind the enlightened citizenry of 1898. He named "Fighting" Joe Wheeler, a Confederate hero, as a major general. When Fighting Joe saw Spanish troops retreating in Cuba, he called out: "Come on, boys, we got them damn Yankees on the run."

The war with Spain was fought in the Philippines, Cuba and Puerto Rico, island remnants of the once-mighty Spanish empire.

Key West, 90 miles from Cuba, was an important strategic location. With a large Cuban population, the city was a hotbed of agitation for independence for Cuba. Fanned by inflammatory political rhetoric and sensational "yellow" journalism, the cause of a free Cuba erupted into a war between a young lion of a nation, spoiling for a fight, and a tired old tiger, preferring to be left alone.

On January 24, 1898, the *USS Maine* left Key West bound for Havana Harbor, ostensibly on a friendly visit – but actually sent to flex U.S. muscles. Three weeks later, the *Maine* blew up in the harbor, killing 268 Americans. To this day no one knows what caused the explosion– but Americans blamed Spain, remembered the *Maine* and declared war.

Army and Navy servicemen and supplies poured into the tiny island of Key West. The town's three-man police force reeled from the rapid arrival of 10,000 soldiers. Street brawls erupted, as well as racial conflicts between black soldiers and white residents.

The biggest problem was thirst. The winter had been a dry one, leaving the island's cisterns low at just the time when an army of drinkers showed up. Barges loaded with

Embarking U.S. troops in Tampa, 1898. (*Florida Photographic Archives*)

100,000 gallons of water were towed to Key West from as far away as St. Petersburg.

The real solution turned out to be plants to distill fresh water from the salt water that surrounded the island. The Navy cranked up an old distillery it had built during the Civil War. Soldiers hurriedly built new plants. By early June the problem was solved. And, naturally, that's when the rains came.

The railroad mogul, Henry Flagler, saw the war as a business opportunity. He successfully lobbied Washington for a large troop encampment in Miami during the summer months, when the population of the resort city dropped to about 1,200.

Troops from nearby Southern states, outnumbering residents by six to one, soon found out why winter resi-

dents didn't hang around for the rainy season. Their tent city offered little protection from the relentless summer heat and the even more relentless mosquitoes.

Soldiers harassed Miami's blacks. Once the entire black community had to flee their homes. Riflemen used coconuts for target practice and others scandalized residents by swimming naked in Biscayne Bay. Anything to cool off.

One soldier summed it up in a letter home: "If I owned both Miami and Hell, I'd rent out Miami and live in Hell."

Lt. Col. Theodore Roosevelt was among the most colorful of the saber-rattlers who set up camp in Tampa, which, thanks to its railroad and deep-water port, became the military's principle point of embarkation to Cuba. Nearly 65,000 troops came to a sleepy city of 12,000, bringing hefty payrolls.

The sumptuous Tampa Bay Hotel, complete with oriental minarets, was headquarters for the hefty General Shafter and his staff and such distinguished war correspondents as Richard Harding Davis, novelist Stephen Crane, writer and artist Frederic Remington, and a reporter from England named Winston Churchill.

Roosevelt was second-in-command of a rollicking group called the Rough Riders. Their membership included cowboys with such names as Cherokee Bill and Rattlesnake Pete, a Harvard quarterback, worldclass polo players and the son of a Pawnee Indian chief. "My men are children of the dragon's blood," said Teddy.

One night the Rough Riders drove their horses through the front door of a popular Cuban restaurant. It became known as "the Charge of the Yellow Rice Brigade." They were not always that well-behaved. A *Tampa Tribune* story reported that "Alice May, keeper of a whorehouse, was shot in the leg and had several bones broken as Rough Riders rioted."

On June 8, 1898, the invasion force sailed for Cuba. In the pivotal battle of Santiago, Teddy Roosevelt and his Rough Riders charged up Kettle Hill. Legend somehow converted Kettle to San Juan Hill but Teddy had no reason to complain. The legend of San Juan Hill rode him into the White House just three years after the war ended in August 1898.

The Spaniards had been driven from the Americas and the U.S.A. had fought and won a two-ocean war. To many it remains a "splendid little war" – little because it lasted only four months, splendid because it established the United States as a world power.

Into the Beach of Palms Rode the "400"

If you want to get from West Palm Beach to Palm Beach these days, you have your choice of three bridges, all designed to carry pedestrians, automobiles and, as far as most Palm Beachers are concerned, as few trucks and buses as possible.

Back in the 1890s for a brief time you could have made the trip via train. Henry M. Flagler, the founding father of South Florida, had extended his Florida East Coast Railway to West Palm Beach in 1894. That same year on Palm Beach he completed construction of the Royal Poinciana, then the world's largest resort hotel, facing Lake Worth.

Two years later he decided to extend a spur across Lake Worth to deposit his illustrious and wealthy guests at the south entrances of the Royal Poinciana and his new ocean-front hotel, The Breakers.

Since "the season" ended on February 22 in those days, the first trip across, on March 14, 1896, must have been quite an event. Only 17 people made the trip, all of them among the leaders of society's "400," all of them among the social elite of Palm Beach in one of its most glorious periods.

Gladys Vanderbilt, the grand-daughter of the famed "robber baron," Commodore Cornelius Vanderbilt, remembered the trip in later years as "like a house party." Twelve years after the brief journey Gladys married Count Laszlo Szechenyi, Hungary's *envoy extraordinaire* to the United States.

Not surprisingly, the Countess Szechenyi, who was the youngest person on the train outlived the other 16, surviving until 1968, a time when many close observers of the Palm Beach social scene felt that it no longer shone with the luster of the 1890s. As one old resort sport, Alexander Phillips, put it, "The '400' has been marked down to $3.98."

The cream of society posing in front of the Royal Poinciana and the train that took them there. The little girl holding the pineapple is Gladys Vanderbilt, March 14, 1896. *(Sam Quincey, Historical Society of Palm Beach County)*

The Tree That Moved While Standing Still

The tree started life some 200 years ago on the shore of Lake Okeechobee. It's been called "Lone Cypress," "Flat-top Cypress" and "Sentinel Cypress."

And it's also known as the tree that moved a half-mile while standing still.

The story begins in 1881, when a wealthy Philadelphian, Hamilton Disston, bought four million acres of mostly swampy land from the state, with the understanding that he would launch a massive drainage program.

One of his earliest projects was Three-Mile Canal, a waterway to connect the Caloosahatchee River and the 750-square-mile lake. This would allow boats to cruise all the way from Fort Myers, cross the lake and make their way up the Kissimmee River to Disston's headquarters in Kissimmee.

Three-Mile Canal entered the lake just south of Lone Cypress. Boatmen on the Okeechobee immediately began using the tree as an "unlighted lighthouse." For 30 years Lone Cypress was the principal navigational aid on the lake, which hosted as many as 500 commercial boats at one time.

By the start of World War I, enough navigational lights and markers had been installed around the lake to permit Lone Cypress to relax and enjoy a well-earned retirement amid familiar surroundings.

But they weren't familiar anymore. Over the years the land around the old tree had changed. Canals were cut, a dike was built along the lake shore, a lock was installed and land was filled in.

Today Lone Cypress sits a full half-mile west of the lake in downtown Moore Haven. It's now on the north shore of the canal, just west of U.S. 27, enjoying its status as a celebrity tree, honored as a state historic site complete with its own official marker.

Lone Cypress, ca. 1900. *(Fort Lauderdale Historical Society)*

The Great Fort Lauderdale Fire of 1912

A fire that burns down your brand-new office building is nothing to laugh at, particularly when this same fire destroys your town's business district.

Still, despite the grim events of June 1-2, 1912, W.B. Snyder and M.A. Hortt managed to keep a sense of humor.

As Fort Lauderdale real estate partners, they were proud of their new office building. So, they asked their new bookkeeper, A.P. Scudder, an enthusiastic photographer, to take their picture standing on the steps of the building.

The next day the steps were all that was left.

"About midnight that night I was awakened by a bright glare shining in my bedroom window," Hortt wrote years later in *Gold Coast Pioneer*. "When I looked out, I could see that the whole business district of Fort Lauderdale was in flames.

"I dressed and rushed uptown to try and save some of the contents of our office, but it was too late."

But not too late for one more picture taken the following day. With an almost debonair sense of humor, Snyder and Hortt stood on the concrete steps again. And once more Scudder snapped the picture.

Scudder's real strength, however, seems to have been in bookkeeping. His pictures were of poor quality. Fortunately, many other pictures remain that capture the magnitude of the destruction.

Most of downtown Fort Lauderdale was gone. Totally wiped out were the Wheeler and Stranahan stores, Everglades Grocery, Fort Lauderdale Pharmacy, Fort Lauderdale *Herald*, Pioneer Realty, Gutchen's Bakery, Jeffries Meat Market, Oliver Brothers Dry Goods Store, A.E. Johnson's Jewelry, Wheeler garage, the post office and, of course, Snyder & Hortt.

Devastation of 1912 fire, looking north across the New River. *(Fort Lauderdale Historical Society)*

W.B. Snyder and M.A. Hortt in front of their office building. *(Fort Lauderdale Historical Society)*

The only downtown buildings still standing were the Fort Lauderdale State Bank, saved by a bucket brigade bringing water from the New River, and the Osceola Hotel, rescued from doom by dynamite, carefully placed to stop the spread of the fire. Ironically, the Osceola Hotel burned to the ground the following year.

Hortt later wrote: "The fire proved to be a blessing in disguise. Beautiful, new fireproof buildings replaced the old wooden firetraps, and they were stocked with more and better merchandise."

Even more to the point, the town council, confronted with the utter futility of depending on fire departments in Miami and Palm Beach, voted unanimously to establish Fort Lauderdale's first volunteer fire department.

Even the Fires Were Grand at The Breakers

Perhaps they should have named the hotel the Phoenix, after the legendary bird that rises from the ashes of its own demise. Instead, the Flagler people called it The Breakers – appropriate enough for a super-deluxe Palm Beach oceanfront hotel.

Besides being a railroad baron, Henry M. Flagler was a builder of grand hotels. His early ads called them "halls of joy."

One of the grandest of these halls was built on the ocean in 1896. First called the Palm Beach Inn, it was renamed The Breakers. It was rebuilt twice after fires, including one in 1903 when it burned to the ground.

The new Breakers lasted until 1925, when a passing motorist noticed smoke pouring from the roof. Two hours later the grand old hotel was once again a smoking ruin.

The rich and famous grabbed their belongings and rushed out to the hotel grounds to watch in dismayed fascination. Sparks from the fire soon ignited the dry March lawn around them and then flew over to the other side of the island to destroy another Flagler inn, the Palm Beach Hotel.

No one was hurt but a thousand people were without a roof. The Flagler people accommodated them at their Royal Poinciana, the world's largest resort hotel.

In less than a year, at a cost of six million dollars, a new seven-story Italian-style palace was completed by 1,200 workers camped in tents on the hotel grounds. Now, more than 60 years later, The Breakers, one of America's few five-star establishments, is still going strong as the jewel of the Flagler-inspired hotels. Camping is no longer allowed.

The Breakers Hotel ablaze, March, 1925. *(Historical Society of Palm Beach)*

The Last Voyage of "Lola"

The New River has changed through the years. It's not as clean or clear as it once was, nor as full of fish.

But as least the whirlpools are gone.

Some 60-70 years ago, whirlpools menaced the unskilled, and even the skilled, boater. One was near Cooley Hammock, one near the Frank Stranahan House, but the biggest of them all was in the river just a little to the west of today's I-95 bridge.

Lawrence Will, a riverboat captain who wrote a number of books on South Florida, left us this colorful account of the I-95 whirlpool:

"And here...the river seemed to go hog wild. This is where Old Master had pulled the plug from the river's bottom. Sometimes wild eddies, gaping skyward, chased themselves about like kittens playing tag. At other times the open-mouthed passengers might behold the whole pool circling round and round. Floating leaves and branches, drawn towards its center, would whirl dizzily and vanish down the vortex. Here even the biggest boat, avoiding the pool's center, was slowed and tossed about, while water in its wake spouted and bubbled as if boiling over a fire."

"Old-timers believed the whirlpools were bottomless. In 1939, long after they ceased to be problems for boaters, the U.S. Army Corps of Engineers measured the area where the big up-river pool had been. Official reading: 37.3 feet in depth.

One account has it that Capt. Scott Holloway's launch *Lola* was lost in one of the whirlpools. Holloway was an experienced boatman who had captained the dredge boat *Everglades* when it was digging canals in the Glades. *Lola*, a 36-foot-long launch, was named for Holloway's wife. In 1912, Holloway was cruising along in his launch, planning to tie it up to a dredge boat which he captained. He overtook the dredge just as it was passing through a whirlpool. Suddenly, the stern of his launch was sucked under. He rushed to the bow, and was saved by an outstretched hand from the dredge. He posted a $100 reward for the recovery of *Lola*, but no trace of the boat was ever found.

What happened to the whirlpools? Probably silting filled them up after the canals were cut back into the Everglades. It's ironic that Holloway, whose work apparently did its bit in ending the terrors of the whirlpools, lost his own boat in the river. His canal digging came too late to save the *Lola*.

The *Lola*, 1910. *(Fort Lauderdale Historical Society)*

The Grounding of "Prins Valdemar"

Clearly the most bizarre contributor to the real estate collapse in Roaring 20's Florida was the *Prins Valdemar.*

A 241-foot barkentine ship, the *Valdemar* was the largest sailing vessel that had ever tried to enter Miami harbor. It was to be towed to the west side of Miami Beach and outfitted as a 100-room hotel ship.

In the early fall of 1926, the big sailboat arrived at the harbor entrance. Pilots held the ship outside for a week, waiting for absolute calm before trying to bring the ship in. They didn't wait long enough.

As the pilots were steering the vessel through Government Cut, *Prins Valdemar* was grounded at the entrance to the turning basin. Then, a sudden brisk northeast wind caught the ship's three tall masts and turned it over on its side.

For nearly a month the *Valdemar* blocked the harbor so completely that nothing bigger than a rowboat could get in or out. Offshore, a hundred ships, carrying 45 million board feet of lumber, waited while builders onshore wondered where they would get the building materials to fuel the boom.

Finally, the U.S. Army Corps of Engineers began to dig an 80-foot channel around the prone ship. But first they had to subject the proud sailing vessel to a final humiliation. With axes and acetylene torches, they removed its masts. It was no longer a tall ship.

As soon as the new channel was filled with ships, a steamer, the *Lakeport,* was grounded. Later, two dredges broke down and the channel was clogged up again. By the time the inlet was finally in good order, the real estate boom had simply lost its steam. But one more shattering blow was still to come.

On September 17, 1926, a hurricane swept out of the Caribbean and smashed into the southeast Florida coast. What little was left of the boom, the hurricane blew away.

Ironically, the only ship to ride out the storm was the refloated *Prins Valdemar.*

Prins Valdemar, grounded in 1926. *(Historical Association of Southern Florida)*

Kidnapping the President-Elect

Try to kidnap a president these days, or even a presidential candidate, and see how fast you vanish in a tidal wave of beefy Secret Service men.

But in 1921, you could not only kidnap a president and get away with it, you could even make him like it. Times were different in Fort Lauderdale in those days.

In November of 1920, Warren G. Harding, a Republican from Ohio, was elected the 29th President of the United States. Since he would not take office until March, the president-elect used part of this open period to relax. In the early winter of 1921 he was on his way to a moderately well-known resort called Miami Beach. To reach his destination via the Intracoastal Waterway, he was due to travel through an even more obscure resort called Fort Lauderdale.

A number of people in Fort Lauderdale thought the time had come to start removing some of that obscurity. Two of them, the colorful, dashing Commodore A.H. Brook and Thomas Stilwell, decided to do something downright spectacular: hijack the next President of the United States.

Brook brought finely honed promotional skills from his years as a successful New York advertising executive to the presidential caper. Stilwell, who would later become the publisher of the Fort Lauderdale *Daily News* and the *Sentinel*, brought excellent connections to the top echelons of the Republican Party – connections so effective that he learned the exact timing and route of the Harding party's southward trip.

As the Harding yacht passed through the Intracoastal, just north of Las Olas Bridge, a large dredge suddenly ran aground, blocking the progress of the presidential party.

Then, from out of nowhere, Commodore Brook's yacht *Kylo* sidled up alongside the Harding yacht and, in a matter of minutes, spirited the president-elect away.

One can imagine the uproar if something like this happened today. But in 1921 everybody treated the kidnapping of the president-elect as the joke it was intended to be. The city fathers entertained Warren Harding in fine style. They even had him play a round on the city's new links, where he shot an undistinguished 110.

Perhaps it was good that Harding had those relaxing moments in South Florida. Nothing much went right for him after he went to Washington. The Teapot Dome Scandal, one of the most prolonged in the country's history, erupted around him, and in 1923 he died under mysterious circumstances.

But at least his place in history is secure. A 1982 *Chicago Tribune* survey of leading historians and political scholars ranked Harding as the worst president this country has ever had.

President-elect Harding, third from left, aboard the *Kylo*. *(Fort Lauderdale Historical Society)*

Mrs. Fuller's Blooming Menace

The delicate lavender blossoms are beautiful, no getting around it. But that's where the good news stops.

The water hyacinth has become one of Florida's biggest headaches. Hyacinths jam canals, rivers and lakes, blocking boats, breaking wooden bridges, clogging up locks and spillways, even killing fish by using up the water's oxygen.

Wrote Lawrence Will, the poet laureate of the Everglades:

"Sometimes those pesky plants would be jammed so tight that a man could walk on them. In 1921 I was operating a passenger boat from Fort Lauderdale to the lake. At the lock gate in Chosen (near Belle Glade) I had barely managed to force the boat through the hyacinth jam. A Seminole tried to follow in his dugout canoe, but the cussed plants closed in and he couldn't make it. The lock tender's sons, Hans and Fritz Stein, hopped down to help, and the three of them, standing on the hyacinths, picked up the heavy boat and shoved it along on top of the plants."

How did the water hyacinth become such a menace?

The problem started in 1884 at the International Cotton Exposition in New Orleans. The Japanese government imported several hundred hyacinth plants from Venezuela to give away as favors.

One plant, unfortunately, wound up with a Mrs. Fuller, who lived in North Florida, near the St. John's River.

She placed the plant in her fish pond. Soon hyacinths were overflowing the pond. Mrs. Fuller started dumping the surplus in the St. John's, little realizing the chaos she would cause.

Water hyacinths double their number every twelve and one-half days. Ten plants can cover an acre in one growing season. Because they are imported, hyacinths are not slowed by Florida's natural checks and balances.

In the late 1890s cattleman Eli Morgan brought some of the St. John's hyacinths to the Kissimmee River area, hoping they might provide cheap feed for his cattle. The plan didn't work because the plants are 96 percent water; cattle can starve to death eating them. So the plants kept spreading, eventually reaching the Everglades.

By 1949 the state was spending as much as ten million dollars a year to fight them. In the 1960s what is now the South Florida Water Management District used munching manatees to try to control the spread of hyacinths. The experiment didn't work for the same reason the flowers didn't work as cattle feed.

Finally, a century after Mrs. Fuller started it, the Great Hyacinth Invasion has finally been halted. With chemicals, the prolific plant, though far from wiped out, is at least under passable control.

Water hyacinths clog a Florida canal, ca. 1925. *(Miami-Dade Public Library)*

The Day the Orange Blossom Special Came to Town

January 8, 1927 was a big day in Broward County. It was the day the Orange Blossom Special hit town.

Over the years, the train would huff and puff its way into legend, first as an East Coast institution, and later as a country music classic, recorded in more than a hundred versions by pickers, fiddlers and singers.

The day the Special arrived in Pompano, Mary Foster, of the Pompano Woman's Club, presented S. Davies Warfield, president of the Seaboard Air Line Railway, with a bouquet of string beans, a bizarre but somehow appropriate gesture from a farming community.

In Fort Lauderdale, Mayor John Tidball led a throng of well-wishers who welcomed the celebrities riding the train. The list included many great names: Nicholas Roosevelt, Percy Roosevelt and Coleman DuPont; famous journalists Arthur Brisbane and C.W. Barron, founder of the *Wall Street Journal;* the financier, E.T. Stotesbury, and the noted gambler, Col. E.R. Bradley.

Florida's most famous architect, Addison Mizner, also made the trip, as did the circus world's Ringling Brothers, John and Charles.

The beautiful people had the ride of their lives, royally entertained by Seaboard. Ironically, one of the people most responsible for the fame of the Orange Blossom Special never rode on it. He was too poor.

In 1938 in Jacksonville, Chubby Wise was a struggling cab driver who also happened to be one of country music's best fiddlers. One night he was drinking with his friend Ervin Rouse, of the Rouse Brothers. "I've been known to pop a cap," says Chubby.

About four a.m. they quit the bars and strolled down to the depot where the Orange Blossom Special sat. Admiringly, they gazed into the windows of the famed flyer.

Then, still restless, they went back home to work on a song that would become *The Orange Blossom Special.*

"I wrote the melody in about 30-40 minutes," recalls Wise. "I gave my half of the song to him, just like I'd give you a cigarette. It turned out to be the biggest fiddle tune ever." And the Rouse Brothers, who wrote the lyrics, got all the credit — although that never bothered Chubby.

In the 1940s Wise and his fiddle joined such legendary bluegrass figures as Bill Munroe, Earl Flatt and Lester Scruggs. A book on country music calls him "the fiddler from Florida whose smooth bowing and flashy effects gave much of the outline to subsequent bluegrass fiddling."

Chubby lives now in Glen St. Mary, in North Florida, and he still fiddles in bluegrass festivals all over the South. The real Orange Blossom Special is long gone — retired in 1953 — but its song lives on.

Orange Blossom Special arrives at Fort Lauderdale station, 1927. *(Fort Lauderdale Historical Society)*

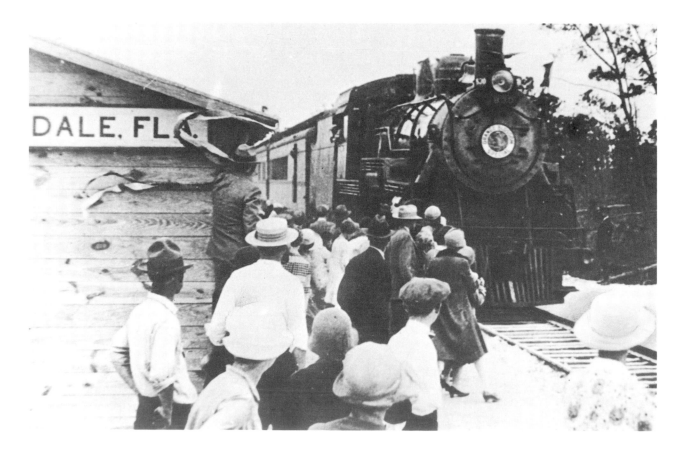

"Booming" Port Everglades

Building a port in Broward County in the depths of a collapsed land boom was considered something of a miracle, and officials of Fort Lauderdale and Hollywood decided that the new harbor rated a noisy sendoff.

Dynamite was selected as the explosive of choice. Picked to set off the charge was none other than President Calvin Coolidge himself.

On Washington's Birthday, 1928, explosives were set to blow away a small earthen dam, which would then open the channel that connected the new port to the ocean. In Washington, the President would detonate the charge by pressing a button.

At the port, virtually the entire population of Fort Lauderdale waited for the explosion. And waited. And waited.

Generally rated as a "do-nothing" president, Silent Cal once again did nothing. Had he forgotten to push the button or had the long-distance relay simply failed?

Finally, engineers at the harbor set off the charge themselves, the crowd cheered and the dedication was declared a success.

For boosters of the port, the wait had been considerably longer. As far back as the 1890s a port had been a dream of community leaders, who wanted Lake Mabel, sometimes called Bay Mabel, reshaped into a turning basin just across from the inlet.

Fort Lauderdale builder Ed King first suggested the idea to railroad baron Henry Flagler, whose Model Land Company owned the lake and the land around it. Later,

in 1913, the Deep Water Harbor Company was incorporated to build the port. The company didn't last out the year.

Eleven years later, during the Florida land boom, developer Joseph W. Young bought 1,440 acres in the name of the Hollywood Harbor and Development Company. He dreamed of a great world seaport to be called Hollywood Harbor.

But the boom collapsed, and with it Young's chances of finishing the job. Near the end of 1927, the First National Bank of Fort Lauderdale informed the Broward County Port Authority it could not honor a BCPA check since it would have left the bank with virtually no funds. The Fort Lauderdale Bank and Trust Company then agreed to take over the troubled bank, providing a home for the authority's deposits.

Six days before the port was due to call on President Coolidge to do the dedication honors, the Fort Lauderdale Bank and Trust Company failed. Lost forever were Post Authority deposits of $151,000.

In all the confusion, the port's first name somehow became Bay Mabel Harbor, which no one liked. A year later, local women's clubs conducted a contest to pick a new name for the facility. The winning entry was the name we still use: Port Everglades.

Crowd gathers for dedication of Port Everglades, 1928. *(Fort Lauderdale Historical Society)*

The Three-Ton Publicity Stunt

Who do you call to caddy for a Republican president-elect? Your friendly neighborhood elephant, naturally. Every golf course should have one.

Carl Fisher had one. He later got a second pachyderm, and used both for much more than carrying clubs. He used them to publicize the swampy sandbar he was busy transforming into Miami Beach.

In 1921 Fisher lured Warren G. Harding to Miami Beach to spend a few sunny days before assuming the presidency. An elephant named Carl II, later renamed Baby Carl, caddied for the politician, and photos of the publicity stunt saturated the United States.

Fisher wrote a friend that he would "get a million dollars' worth of advertising out of this elephant. We are going to...make him tramp down the polo fields between games, also carry trees, haul ice and work in the garden. I have sent to India for a special mahaut (an elephant handler), red cap, brass collar, camel smell and all."

Convincing an elephant to do his bidding proved a difficult task for Fisher. Baby Carl belted him with his trunk, knocked him down and left him black and blue.

Fisher accelerated his search for a Hindu mahaut, skilled in the ways of pachyderms. Unfortunately for Fisher, the conservative tide that had landed his friend Harding in the White House also ushered in a wave of prejudice against letting Asians into the country.

While Fisher's political connections worked overtime to solve the problem, he hired as his mahaut Aaron Yarnell, a lanky Georgian with a knack for handling mules.

After a year, an Indian elephant trainer finally arrived at Ellis Island. But problems set in immediately. The mahaut developed a fever, and the gem merchant who sponsored him became embroiled with the law.

By the time he made it to Miami Beach, the mahaut was exhausted and still burdened with a post-fever smell that offended the sensibilities of Baby Carl. The elephant promptly chased him up a water tank.

The mahaut had to be sent back to India. Yarnell was rewarded by the publicity department with a loftier title, "Chief mahaut from the Bengal plains of Georgia."

Baby Carl was later joined by a little female called Rosie. The two of them, with Yarnell, turned up in countless photos, until Baby Carl, now renamed Nero, had to be sent away to a zoo, leaving behind the gentler and more manageable Rosie.

Once as Yarnell and Rosie were passing a trolley car, Rosie stuck her trunk through an open window, searching for food. The probing trunk awakened a sleeping drunk. Screaming "snakes, snakes," the man leaped off the trolley, breaking his leg. The resulting lawsuit cost Fisher $5,000.

Of Miami Beach's elephant era, Becky Smith, research librarian of the Historical Association of Southern Florida, likes to say: "We're probably the only historical society in the country with an elephant file."

Rosie the elephant in the 1920s. *(Historical Association of Southern Florida)*

Broward's Only Legal Execution

Look beyond the gleaming yachts bobbing in the water at Bahia Mar. Look back to a time when this luxurious Fort Lauderdale marina complex was the site of Broward County's only public execution, and, before that, when it housed a primitive frontier fort in the Second Seminole War.

In 1839, the U.S. Army, busy battling the Seminoles, built a fort on the beach and named it Fort Lauderdale, after Maj. William Lauderdale, who had constructed and commanded an earlier fort on the New River. After the war ended in 1842, the fort was abandoned and allowed to rot.

It was not until 1876 that the government found a use for the land it owned along the beach. That year the United States Life Saving Service authorized the construction of five houses of refuge for shipwrecked sailors along the southeast Florida coast. The Fort Lauderdale House of Refuge was planned for the military reservation where the fort had been.

Lumber to build the refuge was floated ashore from a schooner. Unfortunately, the wood beached not on government property but about a mile and a half to the north. Since it was easier to build it there than transport it down to the reservation, the Fort Lauderdale House of Refuge was built on land the government didn't own.

The House of Refuge filled a very real need. In 1876, virtually no one lived along the southeast coast of Florida. There was no Fort Lauderdale, no Miami, no Palm Beach. Shipwrecked sailors, even if they made it to shore, could starve or die of thirst before finding their way to civilization.

By 1890, the Fort Lauderdale House of Refuge was badly in need of repair. The Life Saving Service concluded that while they were patching it up they might as well move onto government land. By November 1891, the move was completed.

In 1915, the Life Saving Service merged with the Revenue Cutter Service to form the United States Coast Guard. For the remainder of World War I, the Coast Guard took over the operation of the House of Refuge, and in 1926 made the takeover permanent.

Once the South Florida oceanfront was settled, the need for houses of refuge vanished. A shipwrecked sailor who swam to shore in the '20s could expect to find not only food and water, but probably a lively party.

By 1926, the local Coast Guard Base Six had a different foe to battle. In Prohibition days, South Florida Coast Guard stations were kept busy chasing rum runners who cruised over from Bimini and West End in the Bahamas and sneaked in with their illicit cargo through the New River and Hillsboro River inlets.

The Roaring Twenties were light-hearted times, and rum runners were often regarded as dashing, swashbuckling rogues. Then, on August 7, 1927, the rum-running business took an ugly turn.

Horace Alderman. *(Fort Lauderdale Historical Society)*

Coast Guard Cutter 249 had set out for Bimini. On board were a six-man crew and Robert K. Webster, a Secret Service agent who was investigating a counterfeiting ring in the Bahamas. At about one-thirty p.m., the crew stopped a rum boat. The boat operator, Horace Alderman, resisted, drew a .45-caliber pistol and killed Webster, the Coast Guard skipper and the motor machinist, and wounded the cook. Two other crewmen, Hal Caudle of Pompano Beach and Johnny Robinson, subdued Alderman and brought him back to the Fort Lauderdale base.

Alderman was sentenced in Federal Court in Miami to death by hanging. The execution was set for May 11 at the Broward County Courthouse. However, the Broward County Commission objected. They had never had cause to hang a person before, and were not sure how to go about it. Executions, they said, just weren't part of normal county business.

A search of maritime law revealed that a pirate (which the Broward commissioners had determined Alderman to be) *must* be hanged at the port where he was first brought after his arrest. Greatly relieved, the commissioners informed Base Six that it had qualified for the honor of performing the execution, and the hanging was finally scheduled for August 17, at five a.m.

Base carpenters built a 15-foot scaffold at the seaplane hangar, despite the objections of a warrant officer who protested that building scaffolds for hangings was not a proper job for Coast Guard carpenters. And at 6:04 a.m., just as the sun rose over the Gulf Stream he had crossed so often, James Horace Alderman dropped through the scaffold opening. A rum runner, alien smuggler, pirate and murderer, he remains to this day the only person ever legally executed in Broward.

The Killer Hurricane of 1928

Sunday morning dawned cool and overcast over Lake Okeechobee. For some 2,000 people living along the shore of the big lake, this would be their last sunrise.

A monster hurricane, born off the coast of Africa, was bearing down on the lake. It had left more than 900 dead in the Caribbean and had inflicted enormous property damage when it came ashore in Palm Beach County in the early morning hours of September 16, 1928. At West Palm Beach the barometer reading was 27.43, the lowest ever recorded to that time.

It was about noon when people in the lake's farming communities learned for the first time that the storm would strike them. Many migrants living in the shacks and farmhouses in the country received no advance warning at all.

By six p.m., darkness had come and with it the terror of blinding, stinging rain and howling winds. Roofs of houses were blown off, trees uprooted, cars flipped over along the streets. Driven by winds as high as 160 mph, the lake's waters washed away nearly 22 miles of muck dikes along the south shore. The hurricane tide bore down relentlessly.

At Sebring Farm, just east of the Miami Canal, 63 people huddled in the largest farm house. The surging waters destroyed the house; only six people survived.

West Palm Beach at height of hurricane. *(Florida Photographic Archives)*

Near Pelican Bay farther to the east, 34 people took refuge in a dairy barn. All but two were drowned.

Ed King, Fort Lauderdale's first builder, was living on the lake. With 22 others he huddled in John Aunapu's packing house on Torrey Island. Twelve of the 22 died there, including King, struck by a timber while trying to save two children.

When Willie Motes, a Glades trapper, saw people float-

Pompano Theatre after the storm. *(Florida Photographic Archives)*

94

ing past his house, he and his brother started pulling them in until the roomy house bulged with 38 men and women. It was only then that Motes realized that his house, too, was floating. It crossed the Palm Beach road and finally settled, safely, three-quarters of a mile away on the east bank of the Hillsboro Canal.

Author Lawrence Will later wrote: "...huddled on a bit of floating trash and almost touching one another were a kitten, a rabbit and a good-sized water moccasin. By lying flat on the deck I could rescue the kitten while the venomous serpent looked on with apathy, too concerned with his own worries to have any enmity for anyone."

At dawn on Monday, those who survived looked out on an alien landscape. Most of the buildings had been flattened and their familiar world had become a huge lake in which floated the bodies of men, women, children and animals.

How many died in the storm no one knows because no accurate records existed on the number of migrant workers living along the lake. Many of the bodies could not be identified or given a proper burial. For sanitary reasons bodies were piled high and burned. Carpenters were kept busy throughout South Florida, making pine

Aftermath of the storm: stacks of coffins at Belle Glade. (*Florida Photographic Archives*)

boxes. For years after the storm, skeletons were found in the surrounding countryside.

Final estimates placed the death toll between 1,850 and 2,000. To this day, the 1928 hurricane remains the country's third worst natural disaster, exceeded only by the Galveston hurricane in 1900 (which killed 6,000) and the Johnstown flood in 1889, which killed 2,200.

Mass funeral for victims of the storm. (*Florida Photographic Archives*)

Gold Coast Hotels Go to War

Many American GIs saw South Florida for the first time during World War II.

They stayed in the finest hotels and spent long hours on beaches and golf courses – but not doing what tourists do on beaches and golf courses. They were training for the biggest war the world had ever seen.

Thrust suddenly into global conflict, the United States moved quickly to train army troops, airmen and sailors for combat. Time was precious and Sunbelt weather, particularly Florida's, meant intensive outdoor training could be conducted year-round.

One year after Pearl Harbor 147 Miami Beach hotels had become barracks for the Army Air Force Officers Candidate School, Officers Training School and a basic training center.

By the time the war ended one fourth of the AAF's officers and one fifth of its enlisted men had been trained on Miami Beach. More than half a million service men and women learned the basics at one of America's glitziest beaches.

Three months of sixteen and a half hour days turned out officers who were labeled ninety-day wonders. Among the celebrity movie stars trained at Miami Beach were Robert Preston, Gilbert Roland and the biggest matinee idol of them all, Clark Gable.

Offered a major's commission in the Army Air Force, the Great Gable replied: "Hell, I haven't got any more military experience than a chorus girl." He enlisted as a lowly private. He later became a major and flew combat missions.

The hotel where he stayed proudly posted a sign in the lobby which read: "Clark Gable swept here."

In Broward County the Hollywood Beach Hotel

Gas mask drill on Miami Beach. *(Historical Association of Southern Florida)*

quartered Navy officers, while Fort Lauderdale Beach's Tradewinds and Lauderdale Beach Hotels became radar training schools, as did the ritzy Boca Raton Hotel and Club. The Silver Thatch Inn on Pompano's beach provided a home for the United States Coast Guard Mounted Patrol.

After the war ended in 1945, servicemen and women returned to their homes but many restless Americans who had trained in South Florida began to look into the possibility of making it their permanent home. Many in real estate credit this factor as one of the reasons for the startup of Florida's postwar population boom.

For example Fort Lauderdale grew from an estimated 26,185 in 1945 to 83,933 in the Census of 1950. Hollywood's rate of increase was even bigger, from 7,740 to 36,328, while little Pompano moved from 1,027 to 5,682.

Part of the growth was due to pentup demand and postwar prosperity but a big part was servicemen returning to the Gold Coast.

Troops drilling on Collins Avenue, Miami Beach. *(Historical Association of Southern Florida)*

The Day UM Was Sold for $927.23

The University of Miami's football team deals in big numbers. Like the $2.5 million it picked up from the 1988 Orange Bowl game.

In 1946, however, failure to deal properly with some small numbers – namely, $770 in delinquent taxes – brought the university and its football team perilously close to vanishing into a drainage ditch – the kind dug by the Everglades Drainage District.

During its troubled lifetime, the district's mission was to create new farmland by draining the Everglades. Digging canals can be expensive so the district was empowered to levy taxes and sell bonds.

The University of Miami assumed, incorrectly, that its non-profit status brought it immunity from the drainage district taxes. This cozy interpretation placed the university in the same boat as countless other people and organizations who also didn't pay their taxes during the tough days of the Depression.

In 1941, the state legislature decided to help the district recover some of its much needed revenue. An act was passed letting taxpayers bring delinquencies up to date by paying just for the two most recent years. The leniency, however, would end in 1943. After that, tax dodging could lead to loss of the old homeplace.

Most of the land forfeited to the district wasn't worth owning. That is, until 1945, when a closer look at the records revealed a shocker. Wrote Lamar Johnson, district engineer: "One day somebody discovered that the University of Miami belonged to the Everglades Drainage District."

The district didn't want to run a university and it didn't want to put one out of business either. It just wanted its back taxes.

Unfortunately, the law required that the land owned by a delinquent taxpayer had to be advertised for public sale and then sold to the highest bidder. Speculators could have forced the price up or even taken over the university's prime Coral Gables property.

"Why the land speculators did not bid is unknown," Johnson later wrote. It appears, however, that the district worked to keep the procedure as quiet as possible. As a result, UM faced no bidding opposition when it found itself on the auction block.

On February 25, 1946, the University of Miami bought itself back for $927.23 – $770 in back taxes, the rest in interest and costs.

University of Miami, 1930. (*Historical Association of Southern Florida*)

Playing Cupid to Hialeah's Flamingos

Tourists seem to regard the flamingo as the state bird of Florida, for the perfectly natural reason that no matter where you look down here, you run across places named the Flamingo Hotel, or the Flamingo Lounge, or Flamingo Dry Cleaners, or Flamingo Office Supplies, Flamingo Septic Service, and so on.

No thoroughbred race tracks are named after them, but perhaps one should be. Their favorite nesting ground in America is a lushly landscaped tropical sanctuary known to all who have ever made a $2 wager at Hialeah Race Course.

Brought here from Cuba in 1931, the pink birds have made Hialeah their home ever since. The first flamingo ever hatched in captivity was born at the track in 1937.

A hundred years ago flamingos were occasionally sighted around Florida. The arrival of the white man sent them back to the Bahamas and the West Indies. Now one of the few places in America where they will breed is at Hialeah.

In 1972 the birds suddenly stopped breeding. Their traditional breeding season had always come after Hialeah's winter racing dates. But starting in 1972, winter dates were rotated between Hialeah and Gulfstream Park in Hallandale.

For the first time the birds' mating season coincided with a Hialeah racing meet, complete with cheering fans and thundering hoofbeats. The birds were unnerved, and who could blame them? After a few years, they simply forgot how to mate. No eggs were laid, no nests were built. The flock dwindled from more than 600 to less than 400.

Then, in the spring of 1981, a few started pairing off. Angelo Testa, director of operations at the track, concluded they needed all the help they could get. As a boy growing up on his father's New Jersey chicken farm, Angelo had learned to respect the moods and sensitivities of birds. He decided to trick the flamingos into breeding.

The first step was simulated rain. Flamingos mate during or just after rain. Testa mounted sprinkler heads on the tops of 100-foot royal palms.

Mounds were built to remind the birds what a nest looked like. Testa and his son Dennis, who became director of operations, even made plaster-of-paris eggs. Man-made eggs were placed in man-made nests while a man-made rain fell from above. Would the birds remember?

On May 22, 1981, the first genuine flamingo egg appeared. By the middle of June, 51 eggs had been counted. On June 26, the first chick was hatched.

Angelo Testa gave out cigars.

Flamingos at Hialeah Race Course. *(Florida State Archives)*

When Florida Grimly Prepared for War

South Floridians had two things on their minds on October 16, 1962 – the World Series and a tropical storm named Ella that had blown out of the Caribbean.

But far away in Washington, D.C., President John F. Kennedy and a circle of advisors were concerned with something much more ominous. They had just received photographic evidence that Russia was installing ballistic missiles in western Cuba, less than 150 miles from the Florida Keys.

Only a handful of people knew it, but on that day, the world teetered on the brink of nuclear war.

Blissfully unaware, the New York Yankees proceeded to defeat the San Francisco Giants for baseball's championship. Fans who had watched them train each spring at Fort Lauderdale's Yankee Stadium cheered, little dreaming that, before October was over, the stadium would be filled with grim-faced troops.

The Soviets had begun a military buildup in Cuba two months earlier, to improve the island's air and coastal defenses. Concerned, Kennedy warned the Russians against bringing in offensive missiles.

Still, the buildup continued and a U-2 photo-reconnaissance plane was sent to photograph a suspicious area in western Cuba near San Cristobal.

The plane's photos consisted of 4,000 paired and slightly overlapping frames. Photo-interpreters studying the enlarged pictures could read the numbers of license plates 14 miles below. What they identified from these photos was an offensive ballistic missile site.

President Kennedy and his executive committee agreed not to let the Soviets know about the evidence until it could be decided what action should be taken.

While committee members went about the task of

Troops on the ready at Port Everglades, December 1962. *(Gene Hyde Collection, Fort Lauderdale Historical Society)*

Aftermath of crisis, troops drilling at Gulfstream Park, December 1962. *(Gene Hyde Collection, Fort Lauderdale Historical Society)*

developing the U.S. response, South Floridians went about their day-by-day tasks, ignorant of the threat building up 150 miles from their shores.

Wednesday, October 17. Hurricane Ella bypassed the state. At Cape Canaveral, a Minuteman missile went out of control and was blown up. Wreckage rained on the Cape but no one realized how ironically important a subject missiles had become.

In Washington, the president's men were weighing three tough options: bombing the missile sites, invading Cuba or setting up a naval blockade.

Each action had drawbacks. Bombing would kill thousands and still might not destroy all the sites. Also, a bombing run would kill Russian nationals, and Nikita Khrushchev's reaction was unpredictable. He's an impulsive man, warned Ambassador Llewellyn Thompson, just back from Moscow. In a burst of anger, Khrushchev might trigger a nuclear holocaust. Invasion would mean a long, bloody war. Either course was likely to set off the world's first, and probably last, nuclear confrontation. The blockade would not remove the missiles, only prevent more from coming in.

The Russians were moving ahead relentlessly to bring the weapons to combat-readiness. But a blockade did have one big advantage: Once in place, it would force the Russians to think about a face-saving response, somewhere short of World War III.

Thursday, October 18. Key Westers figured that something big was happening. Airborne troops began showing up. The defense department assigned squadrons of the Navy's fastest jet fighters, F4B Phantom Twos, to Boca Chica Naval Air Station.

Said President Kennedy to his advisor Dean Acheson, a former Secretary of State: "This is the week when I had better earn my salary."

Friday, October 19. In South Florida, life went on as normal. Led by quarterback George Mira, Sr., the University of Miami defeated Maryland, 28-24, in a homecoming game at the Orange Bowl.

At Boca Chica, more than 40 C47 cargo planes landed, and the highways were filled with military convoys rolling toward the tip of the peninsula.

Gretchen Morland, who lived on Fort Pierce Beach, just south of Patrick Air Force Base, recalls: "Three nights in a row we saw and heard flights of planes overhead."

Her husband Al had to drive from Fort Pierce to Pompano Beach in time for a chamber of commerce breakfast meeting. "At six in the morning, the turnpike was crowded with convoys, on the way down and on the way back. Trucks, weapon carriers, personnel carriers."

Saturday, October 20. The University of Florida Gators celebrated their homecoming with a 42-7 victory over Vanderbilt.

Farther south, F-100 Supersabre jet fighters were arriving at Homestead Air Force Base. Forty ships and 20,000 men were reported en route through heavy seas toward Puerto Rico, part of "just a routine Caribbean exercise," said the Navy.

The buildup must have impressed Cuban dictator Fidel Castro. He canceled plans for one of his long-winded speeches.

He wasn't the only one who changed his plans that day. JFK's "cold" kept him in the White House. He wasn't sneezing; he was making a tough decision. The United States, he decided, would set up a naval blockade.

Sunday, October 21. Three USAF C119 Flying Boxcars landed at Broward County International Airport, as it was called then. Farther west, tractor-trailers in convoys of five rolled south of US 27, the road to Homestead. A gas station at 20-Mile Bend had a busy day – 60 military trucks stopped for refueling.

In Washington, on a crisp autumn morning, President and Mrs. Kennedy attended Mass at St. Stephen's. That day, the White House worked feverishly, completing preparations for the blockade and for the speech JFK would give the following evening.

Monday, October 22. From Tallahassee, Gov. Farris Bryant alerted all Florida National Guard and Civil Defense units. At Boca Chica, all leaves were canceled. Round-the-clock construction continued on a Key West Airport control tower.

In the western states, 156 Intercontinental Ballistic Missiles were readied for launch. The Strategic Air Command dispersed its B47 and B52 bombers to airfields all over the country in the biggest alert in SAC history.

The Navy had deployed 180 ships in the Caribbean. Five Army divisions were on alert. Author Elie Abel called it "the swiftest, smoothest military buildup in the history of the United States."

At seven p.m., the president began his speech to the nation. Three Miami radio stations and one in Key West beamed his speech to Cuba, revealing for the first time that the U.S. had photographic evidence of the offensive missile sites.

"The purpose of these bases," Kennedy said, "can be none other than to provide a nuclear strike capability against the Western Hemisphere...Several of them include medium-range ballistic missiles, capable of carrying a nuclear warhead for a distance of more than 1,000 miles. Each of these missiles...is capable of striking Washington, D.C., the Panama Canal, Cape Canaveral, Mexico City or any other city in the Southeastern part of the United States..."

The president announced a naval blockade to halt all ships suspected of carrying offensive weaponry to Cuba and demanded that the Soviet Union withdraw all existing offensive weapons from the island.

To make the U.S. stand completely clear, Kennedy added, "It shall be the policy of this nation to regard any nuclear missile launched from Cuba against any nation in the Western Hemisphere as an attack by the Soviet Union on the United States, requiring a full retaliatory response upon the Soviet Union."

Tuesday, October 23. Oliver Lovendahl, Broward's Civil Defense director, received some 20 calls for information on bomb shelters. If it came to war, the county had space for only 5,500 people.

West Palm Beach residents lined the highways to watch B47s, huge KC97 aerial tankers and radar-equipped anti-submarine planes land and take off at Palm Beach International Airport.

One day after the president's speech, Secretary of State Dean Rusk said to his Under Secretary George Ball: "We have won a considerable victory. You and I are still alive."

The Organization of American States voted, 19-0, to back the U.S. position, a powerful endorsement under international law.

Mikhail Polonik, the Soviet delegation's press officer, made an explosive statement to a U.S. information representative: "This could well be our last conversation. New York will be blown up tomorrow by Soviet nuclear weapons."

The test, he said, would come the next day when the first Soviet ship bound for Cuba was scheduled to arrive at the Navy's blockade.

Wednesday, October 24. In Miami, Judge W.R. Culbreath shut down his Juvenile Court and fled to Missouri. The voters were not amused. In the next election they booted him out.

A Miami cab driver was more philosophical: "People ain't running away. Where are they going to run to?"

In Moscow, Khrushchev scowlingly pondered his clash with America's youthful president: "How can I deal with a man who is younger than my son?"

Khrushchev's first move was a cautious one. A dozen Soviet ships turned back.

Said Dean Rusk: "We're eyeball to eyeball and I think the other fellow just blinked."

Thursday, October 25. The Army took over Key West's biggest hotel, the Casa Marina, to house 500 troops in its 167 rooms. Troops also occupied nearby Smathers Beach. Said Ann Davis, a 35-year-old mother who worked as a civilian employee at the naval base: "I'm scared, but I'm not scared enough to run. This is my home and this is where I'm going to stay."

Far away in the Vatican City, Miami's Bishop Coleman F. Carroll, attending the Ecumenical Council, said: "The action of President Kennedy in the quarantine of Cuba was necessary and wise, and representative of the minds of the American people."

In the United Nations' Security Council, the Soviet ambassador challenged UN Ambassador Adlai Stevenson to produce the evidence he said he had. The American answered dramatically: "Do you, Ambassador Zorin, deny that the USSR has placed and is placing medium and intermediate-range missiles in Cuba? Yes or no? Don't wait for the translation, yes or no?...You are in the courtroom of world opinion right now and you can answer yes or no."

"...You will have your answer in due course."

"I am prepared to wait for my answer until hell freezes over."

Stevenson never got his answer, but the Security Council and millions on television saw the photographs of the Cuban missile sites.

Friday, October 26. At the weekly breakfast of the Greater Fort Lauderdale Chamber of Commerce, congressman Paul Rogers reassured the members: "Russia knows the strength of the United States...Day and night they (the Strategic Air Command) have bombers in the air. They have the capacity to obliterate Russia and she knows it."

In Washington, a message outside normal diplomatic channels and a rambling but conciliatory letter from Khrushchev pointed toward a possible breakthrough.

Saturday, October 27. Broward County learned that the military would be taking over Port Everglades as a staging area and a supply facility. Florida congressman William Cramer issued a statement declaring that a Defense Department briefing made it clear that Broward and Palm Beach counties were too close to Cuba to be at risk from the Russian missiles, designed for minimum distances of 350 miles.

Kennedy sent back his reply to Khrushchev. If the Russian leader's response was favorable, the crisis was over. If not, the next move would have to be an air strike followed by an invasion of Cuba.

Said JFK: "Now it can go either way."

Sunday, October 28. Work on Port Everglades was rushed ahead. Construction continued on loading ramps and a railroad spur. Earth movers graded a large area opposite the Florida Power and Light generating station.

In Key West, billowing black smoke from the Boca Chica area startled newsmen and local residents. Nearly 400 people rushed to the site, only to find the fire was across the street from the naval base. The fire's victim was Mom's Tearoom, an abandoned whorehouse.

Shortly before nine on a sunny fall morning, a message arrived at the White House that Khrushchev's reply would be radioed within the hour. The third paragraph contained the good news:

"...the Soviet Union...has given a new order to dismantle the arms which you described as offensive, and to crate and return them to the Soviet Union."

In essence, the Russians had agreed to remove all their offensive weapons and submit the sites to UN inspection in return for an end to the blockade and a promise from the United States not to invade Cuba. The no-invasion pledge gave Khrushchev a way to save face, but no face-saving was provided for Castro. He was completely bypassed throughout the entire negotiations.

The world relaxed, but the U.S. had to stay vigilant. Troops moved into Port Everglades, Yankee Stadium and Gulfstream Park in such numbers that Fort Lauderdale Mayor Edmund Burry sent word to the wire services and 80 major newspapers reassuring the tourist trade that Fort Lauderdale had not been completely taken over by the military.

Advance reservations for the winter season had been heavy. Burry was happy to note that no cancellations had been received. It would be a good season — a season to be thankful that the Cuban missile crisis had not become the start of World War III.

PART FIVE

People Great and Small

The Private War of Mr. Bowles

William Augustus Bowles personally declared war on Spain. Spain won.

Bowles was a soldier and adventurer who came to Florida as a teenager during the Revolutionary War. A native of Maryland, he had teamed up with loyalists and fought for the British.

After the Americans won, he allied himself with the Indian cause. He married the daughter of a Creek chief in northern Florida. And from 1781 until his death in 1805, he took on Spain, which held Florida for most of those years.

Sailing from the Bahamas in the late 1780s, Bowles launched an attack on the Florida peninsula, hoping to cripple the mercantile empire of Panton, Leslie and Co., a Scottish firm that was reaping lush profits by cooperating with the Spanish presence in Florida. Bowles landed near the Miami River and moved north with a small band of Bahamians and Indians, trying to create as much havoc as possible for the Spanish.

After the raid fizzled, some of Bowles' followers returned to settle on the New River. They became the first white settlers in an area that would later become Fort Lauderdale.

In 1789, from London, Bowles wrote the King of Spain demanding that the Indian nations of Florida be given control of their lands, with a port on the Apalachicola River and one at Cape Florida, on Key Biscayne.

If the king would go along with him, Bowles wrote, they could be friends. If not, he threatened to "make war on Your Majesty."

When he returned to America, the Spaniards captured and imprisoned him in Havana, later, he was taken to the Philippines. He escaped, and in his last big effort to strike back at Spain, he established a sovereign nation of Indians, the State of Muskogee. He declared himself "director general."

He issued high-sounding proclamations. Bowles ordered all who held commissions from Spain or the United States off Muskogee soil. He declared the ports of Tampa and Apalachicola open "to all nations that are not at war with us."

His rule as bossman of Muskogee lasted three years. Then, the Spanish offered $4,500 reward for his capture. He was promptly seized.

In jail in Havana, he defiantly refused to have the Cuban governor visit him. "I am sunk low indeed," he said, "but not so low as to receive a visit from the Governor General of Cuba."

It was a grand gesture of defiance but it did him no good. Two days before Christmas, 1805, weakened by a hunger strike, Bowles died in jail at the age of 42.

William Augustus Bowles. (*Florida Photographic Archives*)

Fort Lauderdale's Forgotten Founder

Camp Powell doesn't have quite the same ring to it as Fort Lauderdale. It just doesn't sound like a world-class resort city, but maybe it would if the name had stuck.

A U.S. Navy lieutenant named Levin Powell built a camp on the New River before Maj. William Lauderdale erected his fort during the war against Florida's Indians in 1838. Powell just didn't have the good luck to eventually have a city named after him.

Powell, a native of Virginia, was a career officer, reaching the rank of rear admiral after the Civil War. During the Second Seminole War, which started in late 1835, Lt. Powell developed a new concept, "riverine warfare," using small-boat assault tactics against what was essentially a

guerilla enemy. Powell moved his forces by rowboat into bays, rivers, and the Everglades.

In the fall of 1836, he ventured into the New River with a detachment of about 150 sailors and marines. At the fork of the river he established what has been described as a "strong camp," probably nothing more than a large, well-guarded cluster of tents.

From this first "Camp Powell," he and his forces roved the country-side, looking without success for Seminoles. Their guide was William Cooley, whose family had been massacred on the New River the previous January. Then, for more than a year, Powell ranged up and down the Atlantic coast.

In the late winter of 1838 he was dispatched again to the New River to support Lauderdale's command.

Major Lauderdale had arrived on the river on March 5 and begun constructing his fort on the north bank near the fork. Powell, arriving three days later with 152 sailors and soldiers, set up his second Camp Powell just across from Fort Lauderdale on the south side of the river.

Troubled by respiratory illnesses, Lauderdale returned to his native Tennessee and died later that spring. But his name lives on, adopted in 1911 as the new city's name.

Powell lived until 1885, his name virtually forgotten, but not the riverine war tactics he had developed. More than a century later, American soldiers would use them in the jungles of Vietnam.

A Civil War photo of Lt. Levin Powell, *(Fort Lauderdale Historical Society)*

Waiting Out the Civil War in Palm Beach

Palm Beach is home today to many rich and famous personages – some of whom would prefer to keep a low profile. Its first resident also used the secluded island as a hideaway from the Civil War.

His name was August Lang. Although a native German, he did his bit for the South by disabling the Jupiter Lighthouse. He then hid out, apparently fearing arrest by U.S. coastal patrols.

Lang lived unnoticed until 1866, when the War was over and the Florida sea lanes were open again.

That fall, Michael Sears and his son set out in a small schooner from their home on Biscayne Bay. They sailed north to the Indian River.

Returning after several weeks of heavy rain, they spied an opening in the beach ridge that hadn't been there earlier. They sailed through and found themselves on the waters of today's Lake Worth.

They soon saw a small cabin in a clearing on the east side of the lake. A man came out to greet them, and asked how the war was going.

"War?" replied Sears. "What war?"

"Why, the War between the States, of course," said Lang. "The fighting's been over for more than a year."

By 1886, the location Lang picked to wait out the war had become the town of Palm Beach. The site he settled would become the grounds for the home of Sanford Cluett, who was immortalized by his development of an anti-shrinkage process for men's shirts. It was called Sanforizing.

But Lang never lived to see those things. With the war over, he and his wife moved north, near today's Stuart. There, he was shot to death by three Florida crackers, who proceeded to cut his body up and stuff the pieces into an alligator hole. One of the three suspects was shot by the sheriff, the others were arrested.

The most noteworthy thing about the trial was the defense employed by suspect Tom Drawdy. His attorney based his case on the jurors' fear of ghosts, arguing that hanging an innocent man would leave them haunted by his spirit.

What was the result? One account says Drawdy was acquitted, the other that he died in prison.

Drawing of August Lang, ca. 1870. (*Historical Society of Palm Beach County*)

Metcalf's Newspaper Covered Melbourne to Miami

The first newspaper to serve South Florida followed the path of Henry Flagler's railroad, but it didn't always follow his party line.

Guy Metcalf, a 21-year-old journalist from Ohio, began his Florida publishing career by founding *The Indian River News* in Melbourne (near today's Cape Canaveral) on Feb. 24, 1887. But as Flagler's Florida East Coast Railway came south, so did the newspaper. Metcalf moved the paper first to Juno, changing its name to *The Tropical Sun,* and in 1895 relocated again to West Palm Beach after the railroad reached the new city on Lake Worth.

In those days, *The Tropical Sun* was the only newspaper on the southeast Florida mainland (Key West, the major population center, had its own newspapers). It had a huge circulation area – stretching from Melbourne to Miami – but few readers. Settlements had but handfuls of hardy souls.

Metcalf's motto, proudly displayed at the top of page one, read: "Search for the Truth is the Noblest Occupation of Man, Its Publication a Duty."

Frequently Metcalf's "duty" led him to tangle with the mighty magnate who developed southeastern Florida.

For example, in 1901 the Florida legislature passed the "Flagler Divorce Law," which made incurable insanity grounds for divorce in Florida. The only person to use it before it was repealed was Flagler – and Metcalf delighted in blasting him for it.

So deep was Flagler's enmity toward Metcalf that the publisher is generally given as the principal reason that Flagler chose not to be buried in Palm Beach.

The Tropical Sun was usually a cheerful, down-home paper. One of its correspondents was E.R. Bradley, a barefoot mailman and later superintendent of Dade County Schools. He wrote columns on neighborhood news, using three different names: "Ruthven," his middle name, "The Sage of Lotus Cove," a reference to the site of his Lantana home, and "O.M.B.," which stood for "Old Man Bradley."

Metcalf was a community go-getter as well as a publisher. One of his projects was building the county road from Lantana to Lemon City, now a part of Miami. Bridges were built over all the streams along the way except for the deepest of the waterways, the New River. There he installed a ferry and a camp for overnight visitors.

To run the ferry and camp, Metcalf brought down from Melbourne a cousin and fellow Ohioan. That man was Frank Stranahan, who stayed on to become the founder of modern Fort Lauderdale.

Guy Metcalf, ca. 1890. *(Fort Lauderdale Historical Society)*

The World's Greatest Librarian

Steel Tycoon Andrew Carnegie earned lasting fame for his support of libraries. The Scotsman endowed 2,509 free public libraries in the English-speaking world, 1,679 of them in the United States.

In South Florida, his wife Louise beat him to the punch. On a yachting trip to Biscayne Bay in the 1890s, she stumbled upon a meeting of the Pine Needle Club, a Coconut Grove literary society. On her return north she shipped back bundles of books. Her shipment was the start in 1895 of the Coconut Grove Library.

Fourteen years earlier, Carnegie had endowed his first library – in his home town of Dunfermline, Scotland. When he was 13, his family moved to the Pittsburgh area where a free library system helped him educate himself. A successful career in railroading led him into the emerging steel industry, which would make him the world's second-richest man.

Carnegie would easily have become America's first billionaire, but a funny thing happened on the way to the top: He started giving his money away. The steel magnate believed that anyone who had accumulated a vast fortune should redistribute a substantial part of it for the good of society.

He distributed roughly 90 percent of his earnings of $350 million to worthy causes – including peace, education, and a hero's fund. He gave most enthusiastically to libraries because, as he put it, "The library gives nothing for nothing...it helps only those who help themselves."

Carnegie was one of a number of wealthy Pittsburghers who sought the warm climes of Palm Beach.

The first of them was Commodore Charles J. Clarke, who donated a large houseboat to the Palm Beach Literary Society for a library. Others included principals of the Carnegie Steel Company: Andrew Carnegie, his brother, and Tom and Henry Phipps. The Phipps family eventually became the largest land owner in Palm Beach; at one time the largest holders of prime real estate on the East Coast of the United States.

Carnegie left his stamp on Florida in a different way. Ten of the libraries he endowed were in Florida cities – Bartow, Bradenton, Clearwater, Gainesville, Ocala, Jacksonville, Palmetto, St. Petersburg, Tampa and West Tampa.

Andrew Carnegie and his wife, center, in Palm Beach, ca. 1890s. *(Historical Society of Palm Beach County)*

122 Years of Tall Tales

Somehow Old John Gomez made it into the 20th century, quite a feat for a man who said he was born in 1778 in Portugal – or was it the island of Mauritius?

There was usually a fair amount of confusion when Gomez started telling his tall tales. But he was believed to be the oldest man in the United States until he drowned on July 12, 1900, near Panther Key, just south of Marco Island.

A fisherman in his later years, Old John may have caught his foot on the anchor line or the net and been dragged overboard. Or, some suspect, he might have committed suicide. He had become tired of living, explained his 94-year-old wife.

Well, he *had* lived a long time – 122 years. And to hear him tell it, it had certainly been a full life.

His eventful career, he said, brought him into contact with world leaders. As a boy he had been patted on the head by Napoleon. As an older man, he claimed to have fought in the Second Seminole War. At the Battle of Lake Okeechobee on December 25, 1837, he served under the command of Zachary Taylor, who would later be elected President of the United States.

What really drew attention to Gomez, though, was his account of his days as a pirate. He sailed, he said, with a buccaneer Jose Gaspar, better known as Gasparilla.

Gasparilla is reported to have terrorized the Gulf Coast of Florida in the early 1800s. Legend has it that the bloody reign came to an end in 1822 when he was trapped by an American warship. Rather than face the hangman he wrapped an anchor chain around his waist and drowned himself in the waters near Boca Grande Pass.

With his buccaneer days behind him, John Gomez herded cattle for a while near Cedar Key, then operated as a blockade runner during the Civil War.

Finally he settled on one of the Ten Thousand Islands on Florida's southwest coast. He called his island Panther Key because he tried to raise goats there, but the panthers kept eating his stock.

Then, in 1884, at age 106, he married a 78-year-old woman he met while on a trip to Tampa, and took her back to his remote island.

For a hermit he attracted a fair number of visitors. People who had heard his Gasparilla tales descended upon Panther Key to dig for treasure. Writers from such national publications as *Forest and Stream* called often to weave stories from his fanciful yarns.

Still, it was never a good idea to underestimate Gomez. Around 1890 a man named Sampson Brown offered to build the centenarian a house from the timbers of a wrecked ship, with the proviso that Old John would will the island to him upon his death. Brown was in his 50s, Gomez over 110. Old John outlived Brown by eight years.

John Gomez and his wife on Panther Key, ca. 1890.
(Collier County Museum)

The Martyrdom of Marti

In appearance he was not an impressive man. He was pale, thin and tense. His mustache drooped and his hairline receded.

But when Jose Marti spoke, crowded factories and convention halls fell silent. His oratory, some said, could "wring tears from a corpse."

Born in Havana in 1853, Marti grew up on an island which lived under Spanish rule. He was a rebellious youth. When he was only 16, his legs were manacled with chains for advocating Cuban independence.

Deported to Spain, Marti earned three university diplomas and began to realize that he was blessed with a gift for public speaking.

He learned English, convinced that his base of operations would have to be the United States. That was where Cuban exiles were keeping alive the dream of a free homeland.

In 1891 he came to the U.S., visiting New York and the two Florida cities where the exiles were concentrated – Tampa and Key West, then the state's most populous city. His greatest support came from the cigar makers. Many of them gave him 10 percent of their earnings.

By 1892 Marti had organized a chain of local organizations into the new Cuban Revolutionary Party. Key West alone had 61 freedom clubs, Tampa 16. At that time there was no Miami.

In Key West he would speak at the home of Teodoro Perez at Duval and Catherine Streets. Perez owned a cigar factory and served as secretary of the Cigar Manufacturers Union.

(The house where Marti visited still bears his name. Now a pink-hued guest house and restaurant, it is called La Terraza de Marti, better known as La Te Da.)

At a gathering of Cuban exiles in Tampa, Marti declared, "I should want the cornerstone of our Republic to be the devotion of Cubans to the full dignity of man. Either the Republic has as its foundation...the unrestricted freedom of others – in short, the passion for man's essential worth – or else the Republic is not worth a single one of the tears of our women nor a solitary drop of a brave man's blood."

In 1895 it was the blood of Marti himself that was shed. Returning to Cuba to join the troops fighting Spain, he was killed one moonlit evening in a surprise attack by the Spaniards.

Jose Marti lived only 42 years, not long enough to see Cuba win her independence from Spain. Nearly a century after his death, Cuba's greatest national hero lends his name to still another effort to gain freedom for Cuba. It is the U.S.-funded, anti-Communist broadcasting station called Radio Marti.

Jose Marti, second from right, behind child, Key West, 1892.
(Historical Association of Southern Florida)

The Women Who Saved Paradise Key

In 1893, the dean of the University of Florida College of Agriculture and the director of the New York Botanical Garden sloshed their way through the waters of the Everglades till they reached a mile-wide hammock.

The two men had heard about the hammock, which enjoyed a modest fame for its magnificent stand of royal palms growing wild. Their photographs of lush tropical vegetation prompted the first calls to preserve the area.

Over a half-century later, Paradise Key would become an important step in the establishment of Everglades National Park. But it took a group of determined women to make it happen.

Most of the land near Paradise Key belonged to the Model Land Company, the real estate arm of the vast Florida empire created by railroad king Henry Flagler.

Amid rumors that buyers were interested in the land for development as citrus groves, J.E. Ingraham, a top Flagler executive, met with Mary Barr Munroe, chairman of the Florida Federation of Women's Clubs to discuss the future of the hammock.

Mrs. Munroe, wife of the novelist Kirk Munroe, was a fiery activist. To protest women wearing egret plumes on their hats, she was known to walk up to total strangers and suddenly and violently yank the hats from their heads.

The results were spectacular, especially when the hats were pinned to the women's hair.

If she wasn't afraid to attack the heads of fashionable women, Mary Munroe certainly wasn't going to be shy about telling Ingraham what she wanted: the donation of Paradise Key to the Federation to preserve a park.

Ingraham agreed with her, and managed to persuade Mary Lily Kenan Flagler, Henry's widow, to give nearly a thousand acres to the federation. The state matched it with an additional thousand acres.

On Nov. 22, 1916, Ingraham Highway, the road the Model Land Company had built to the hammock, carried 150 automobiles filled with 750 people to the dedication of Royal Palm State Park.

The first caretaker, Charles A. Mosier, lived with his family in a tent for three years until the completion of a lodge to house and feed visitors to the park.

Despite fire and the hurricane of 1926, the Women's Club kept the park going until it was taken over by the federal government in 1947.

Charles Torrey Simpson, left, and Charles Mosier at Royal Palm Lodge, ca. 1920. *(Historical Association of Southern Florida)*

112

The Gunrunner Who Became Governor

With a name like Napoleon Bonaparte Broward, the man had to be a peerless leader and a dashing character.

Broward, for whom the newly-created county was named when oversized Dade County was split up in 1915, first demonstrated his leadership as sheriff of Duval County, then as governor of Florida. He was a U.S. Senator-elect when death claimed him in 1910. He was 53.

A little known chapter of Broward's daring career was a stint as a gunrunner.

With two of his friends, Broward had bought a powerful, ocean-going tug, which the three of them imaginatively named *Three Friends*. Their plan was to engage in towing and salvaging and to ferry cargo and passengers from Jacksonville to Nassau.

However, in Cuba, rebels were beginning their struggle to break free from the rule of Spain. Sympathy in South Florida was strongly on the side of the rebels.

Typically, Broward backed up his sympathies with action. He ran guns and supplies to the rebels and transported Cuban patriots to and from the island nation, despite federal laws proscribing both actions.

The tug's captain was "Dynamite" Johnny O'Brien, a former New York harbor pilot. He earned his colorful nickname from a voyage in which he transported 60 tons of dynamite across the Caribbean, prevailing against a hurricane, a severe electrical storm and a crew that became hysterical when they learned the true nature of their cargo.

It was believed that Broward used to tie up *Three Friends* at Frank Stranahan's docks on the north side of the New River, near where the Fort Lauderdale tunnel is today. But no one is sure. Gunrunners were not in the habit of making their whereabouts well known.

Gun running was a lucrative business, but it had its risky side. If a Navy ship had caught Broward on a gunrunning mission, he would have been subject to fines, imprisonment and forfeiture of his boat. If the Spanish had caught him, it would have meant the firing squad.

Broward's Cuban exploits led to his election as governor in 1906. Some time later, he was talking to President Theodore Roosevelt, another hero of the Cuban revolution. Roosevelt asked Broward if he still owned the *Three Friends*. Broward said yes.

"Well, you ought to be mighty proud of her," the president said. "If it had not been for *Three Friends*, you would not be governor now."

"You ought to be proud of her yourself," replied the governor, "because if it had not been for her, you would not be President of the United States."

The Three Friends, 1890s. *(Fort Lauderdale Historical Society)*

Remington's Last Roundup

He was America's most famous painter of the Old West. But where was he to go when the Old West was gone?

Frederic Remington went to Florida, and he didn't like what he saw. He favored cowboys of heroic stature and deeds, acting out the legends of the West against a backdrop of rugged mountains, deserts and canyons. He didn't find any of these in the scrub lands of Florida.

On assignment in 1895 to write and illustrate a story about "cracker cowboys" for *Harper's Weekly*, Remington found a flat, sandy land which he described as "truly not a country for a high-spirited race or moral giants." The cattle, he said, were "scrawny creatures not fit for a pointer-dog to mess on."

Fortunately, it was Remington's pictures, not his words, that lived on. He captured on canvas a priceless interpretation of life among the cowhunters (as they were called then) who plied their trade in the grazing lands west of Lake Okeechobee.

Later Remington came to Key West and Tampa to paint scenes of a young nation girding for its first overseas war – the Spanish-American War of 1898, in which Cuba was a major battleground.

But even then, it was the words of his publisher, William Randolph Hearst, which found a larger place in history. Hearst's *New York Journal* was whipping up a pro-war frenzy while Remington was patiently waiting in Havana for the conflict to begin, so he could send back illustrations. The artist wired Hearst: "Everything is quiet. There is no trouble. There will be no war. I wish to return."

Hearst's reply: "Please remain. You furnish the pictures and I'll furnish the war."

Despite his forays into Florida and Cuba, Remington will always be associated in the art world with romanticized scenes of cowboys, Indians, cavalrymen, trappers, mountain men, horses and buffalo. As one art critic wrote: "There is no other name which symbolizes our wild Old West as does Frederic Remington."

Ironically, Frederic Sackrider Remington was very much an Easterner. Born in 1861 in Canton, N.Y., he attended the Yale School of Fine Arts and starred as a running back for the Yale football team.

Two Florida cowboys painted by Remington in 1895.
(Florida Photographic Archives)

When he was 20, he sought the hand of Eva Caten in marriage. Her father said no, and a broken-hearted Remington went West to forget his troubles. There he found the outlet for his considerable talents, both as an artist and writer.

Remington was lucky in his timing. He was painting his pictures at a time when American magazines had just gained the technology to reproduce paintings and watercolors effectively.

The result was a strong demand for illustrations, so strong that Remington soon became a famous and successful man. He was even able to marry his sweetheart Eva, and he spent most of the 1880s venturing forth

Bone Mizell, Remington's *Cracker Cowboy. (Florida Photographic Archives)*

from his home in upper New York state to paint scenes of the West.

But eventually the Old West faded away. In 1890 the massacre at Wounded Knee marked the last big clash between the U.S. Army and the Indians. That same year the federal census indicated that virtually no frontier remained in the West.

The culprit, Remington concluded, was the wire fence. America, he said, had seen the end of "the cowboy – the real thing, mark you, not the tame hired man who herds cattle for the mere wage of it."

After 1894 Remington made no more major painting expeditions into the West. He worked instead from memory and previous sketches in his studio in New Rochelle, N.Y. Then came the *Harper's* assignment that took him to Florida's cow country, a vast, sprawling land unhampered by the wire fences he hated.

Arcadia, Florida, could have passed for a western cow town with its wooden sidewalks, dirt streets, and horse troughs in front of the stores. Cattle had been raised in southwestern Florida since the Spanish introduced livestock in the early 1500s, but the industry had none of the heroic trappings Remington found in the Great Plains. Standing outside an Arcadia store, he was jolted by this scene:

"Two very emaciated Texas ponies pattered down the street; bearing wild-looking individuals, whose hanging hair and drooping hats and generally bedraggled appearance would remind you at once of the Spanish moss which hangs so...helplessly to the limb of the oaks out in the swamps. There was none of the bilious fierceness and rearing plunge which I had associated with my friends out West...

"The only things they did which were conventional were to tie their ponies up by the head in brutal disregard, and then get drunk in about 15 minutes."

The contrast was just too much for Remington. He loved mountains, valleys and open range, tumbleweed and purple sage. What he got was palmetto bushes and sawgrass.

And instead of heroic figures, he found a character named "Bone" Mizell.

For some reason Remington chose Morgan Bonapart Mizell as the model for one of the most famous of his Florida pictures, *A Cracker Cowboy.* Bone was a hard-drinking, hard-riding, hard-living cowboy who had been known to light his pipe with dollar bills. Once he rode into a saloon and his first drink before dismounting from his horse.

Bone was top hand with cattle baron Ziba King's outfit along the Peace River, a crack shot with a rifle or a six-shooter.

But he was hardly the type of macho cowboy that Remington admired. Bone was a joker, a man whose lisp brought ridicule. He covered his embarrassment with a quick, sharp wit.

Bone was a heavy drinker of a cheap and potent booze called Jamaica ginger. Once, after he passed out in a saloon, his cowpoke pals dumped him in a graveyard, built a circle of fire around him and poked him with sticks to wake him up. "Dead and gone to hell, 'bout what I expected," said Bone.

It's a wonder that Remington ever came back to Florida after spending a few weeks with Bone and company. But the opportunity to chronicle a war proved to be attraction enough. To his old friend, Owen Wister, the noted author of westerns, Remington remarked: "We are getting old and one cannot get old without having seen a war."

In the 1890s, Cubans were rebelling against Spanish rule. Hearst commissioned Remington and the famed war correspondent, Richard Harding Davis, to cover the rebellion for his *New York Journal.*

Remington and Davis traveled to Key West. Unfortunately for them, the Spanish Navy's blockade of Cuba stymied their three attempts to run the blockade in Hearst's powerboat. Remington had to remain in Key West for three weeks.

In later years artists would find the island city picturesque and stimulating. Remington detested Key West. He called it a "dusty, smelly bit of sandy coral, and the houses are built like snaredrums; they are dismal thoroughly, and the sun makes men sweat and wish to God they were somewhere else."

After failing to breach the blockade. Hearst's dynamic duo finally made it into Havana in January, 1897. Their method was less than swashbuckling. They simply took a regularly scheduled steamer.

Alas, they found no military action. Totally bored, Remington sent the wire to Hearst saying so. And Hearst promised to "furnish the war."

Another year would go by before the *Maine*, a U.S. battleship sent to protect American property and lives in Cuba, exploded in Havana harbor. The press blamed Spanish agents, and by April, 1898, President McKinley declared war.

Remington found himself back in Florida, this time in Tampa. The West Coast city served as a major staging area for American soldiers and boats bound for war. Remington didn't like Tampa, either. He called it a place "chiefly composed of derelict houses drifting on an ocean of sand."

Finally with the U.S. Fifth Corps he got his chance to see war first-hand. Remington was there at the Battle of San Juan Hill when his friend and admirer, Teddy Roosevelt, galloped into history with his Rough Riders.

It should have been a memorable moment for Remington. Actually, the reality of combat proved far removed from his romanticized dreams. The suffering and death at every turn, the heat, the danger and, finally, a bout with yellow fever, cured him of his taste for war. He returned to the United States.

Said Remington: "From now on I mean to paint fruits and flowers."

Broward's First Family

Philemon Nathaniel Bryan arrived in Fort Lauderdale from North Florida in 1895, riding Henry Flagler's Florida East Coast Railway. He and his sons, Tom and Reed, had been hired by Flagler to supervise the 400 laborers who were laying the stretch of track that finally brought the FEC to the New River.

Adapting easily to their new hometown, the Bryans soon had a hand in nearly everything. It was Philomen's brother, Gadsden ("Gad"), who established Fort Lauderdale's first saloon, on the banks of the New River.

Gad later gained some notoriety by training nine Seminoles for a "Wild South Show." Gad shaved his head and billed himself as "The Bald-Headed Seminole of the Everglades."

Meantime, Philomen built Fort Lauderdale's first hotel, just west of the new railroad tracks. His second hotel still stands, known today as the Discovery Center.

Reed Bryan was hired by Governor Napoleon Bonaparte Broward to build two dredges to start the digging of the first canals in the governor's Drain-the-Everglades program. The mammoth machines were built on the south side of the river, across from Reed's home, where Shirttail Charlie's Restaurant now stands. Reed's home and that of his brother, Tom, were later linked and became the Historic Bryan Homes Restaurant.

According to grandson Jimmy Bryan, Reed owned the first automobile in Fort Lauderdale, a Glider with 42-inch wheels. Brother Tom owned the first seaplane. Tom also started the first power company, called for some reason the Fort Lauderdale Ice and Light Company, the first phone company and the first radion station, WFTL. He was also instrumental in getting a large hunk of what was then Dade County renamed Broward, after the governor who had hired his brother, Reed.

Philemon's half-brother, Frank A. Bryan, was chairman of the county commission for Dade County. When Broward was formed in 1915 he became the new county's first clerk of court.

By coming early, staying late and leaving their imprint all over the county, the Bryans are the most logical choice for the title "Broward's First Family."

The Bryan Family in 1921. From left, standing, Tom and Camille Bryan, Perry Bryan, Florence Bryan Barrett, Constance Bryan Gardner, Stella and Reed Bryan. Seated, Lucy Murray Bryan and Philemon N. Bryan. Children in front, James Bryan, Reed A. Bryan, Jr., and Betty Bryan. *(Fort Lauderdale Historical Society)*

Yellow Jack and the Little Doctor

Fort Lauderdale's first doctor parlayed a yellow fever epidemic and a government probe into a medical degree.

North Carolinian Tom Kennedy picked up a knowledge of medicine as an army medic and as a watchdog for the hopelessly insane second wife of railroad tycoon Henry Flagler.

Kennedy was hired, he later wrote, "to watch the Flagler residence...so if Mrs. Flagler became violent or got away from the nurses, I could assist them. I had nothing to do but keep in calling distance of the house, so I almost memorized Flint's *Practice of Medicine*. I studied it the whole time I was on the job."

In 1899 Kennedy came to Fort Lauderdale to raise tomatoes. Later that year one of the local pioneers returned from Miami suffering from jaundice, vomiting and a high fever. Kennedy recognized the symptoms of yellow fever, the dreaded "yellow jack."

Virtually everybody in the little New River community caught the disease. Kennedy had no choice. He had to do everything he could to save the lives of his neighbors. He tended his tomatoes, then traveled up and down the river, administering calomel, epsom salts and quinine.

When the disease finally ran its course, Fort Lauderdale was the only South Florida community to escape without a fatality.

Kennedy went back to his tomato farm west of Flagler's Florida East Coast railroad tracks.

Then, one day, two doctors from the U.S. Bureau of Health showed up. Some snitch had informed the government that Kennedy was practicing medicine without a license.

He answered the charges at a government hearing. The board listened to his account of what happened, then reached a remarkable conclusion.

The board ruled that not only should he be cleared of all charges but that he should be paid for the services he had rendered. Tom Kennedy used the check they gave him to finance a medical degree from the University of the South.

In 1901 he returned to Fort Lauderdale to practice medicine – with a license. Only five feet five, he would be known for many years as the "Little Doctor." Once after treating a patient in Delray Beach, Dr. Kennedy started to walk home. He passed out from the heat near the FEC tracks. When Henry Flagler heard of the incident, he passed the word along to his railroad employees: "When the Little Doctor needs to go anywhere, take him."

Dr. Tom Kennedy, ca. 1910. *(Fort Lauderdale Historical Society)*

"Birdie" and Friends in Palm Beach, 1907

When Virginia Fair Vanderbilt visited a Palm Beach photo studio in 1907, she proved to be the center of attention.

Ernest Histed, the photographer, seated Virginia, also known as "Birdie," in a conveyance called a Palm Beach Chariot or, in those insensitive times, an afromobile, because the pedal power was usually supplied by a black servant.

In the picture the power spot was held by Lawrence Waterbury, a friend of the family. On each side of the vehicle were Leland Sterry, manager of The Breakers Hotel, and brother Fred, manager of the Royal Poinciana Hotel.

Birdie's husband, William K. Vanderbilt, was given a stuffed alligator to hold, a prop he found amusing.

Snaring a Vanderbilt was quite an achievement for Birdie, a social climber from San Francisco. The Vanderbilts were the highest of high society.

Birdie's father Jim, sometimes called "Slippery Jim," has been described as a black-bearded, brooding, cheating, loud-mouthed, lying, drunken, belligerent Irishman.

These drawbacks, however, could be overlooked. After all, he was extraordinarily wealthy, the result of his part ownership of the fabled Comstock Lode in Nevada, one of the richest veins of gold and silver ever found.

Jim Fair had one particularly nasty habit. He liked to make fools of people. He would recommend worthless mining stocks, knowing that people would buy them on his say-so.

Once he even pulled a trick on his wife. She had asked him about a good stock. He picked one, cautioning her not to tell anyone. He knew, of course, that his talkative wife would tell her friends. Mrs. Fair and her friends lost a small fortune.

Fair reimbursed her for her loss. He told her it should be a lesson for her. It was. She divorced him.

Birdie and her sister, Teresa, lived with their mother. Like Birdie, Tessie had the good fortune to marry into a society family, the Oelrichs. Jim Fair was not invited to either wedding.

Willie Vanderbilt, an auto racing enthusiast, sponsored races and is sometimes credited with popularizing the sport in America. He and Birdie were later divorced, leaving him free to cruise around the world on his two and one-half million dollar yacht.

One monument to Jim Fair still stands in San Francisco. It is the Fairmont Hotel, the hostelry TV viewers see each week at the beginning of the series *Hotel*.

"Birdie" Vanderbilt in afromobile, center, Palm Beach, 1907. *(Ernest Histed, Historical Society of Palm Beach County)*

119

Carry Nation in South Florida

Early this century, a cyclone blew into South Florida in the person of Carry Nation.

Saloons everywhere were terrorized by the "Kansas Cyclone." A towering, six-foot figure in black, she strode unafraid into the dens of the sinful, armed with bricks, a hatchet and her Bible.

At the invitation of the local chapter of the Women's Christian Temperance Union, Carry Nation came to Miami in 1908. At a meeting in a gospel tent she told the assembled throng: "The same God that put a staff in Moses' hand, a jawbone in Samson's hand, a sling in David's hand, put a hatchet in Carry Nation's hand."

Carry had first earned her reputation as a hatchet-wielding bar buster back in Kiowa, Kansas. In 1900 she stormed into a bar there and announced, "Men, I have come to save you from a drunkard's fate!"

Then she cut loose with bricks and stones, shattering the mirror behind the bar and breaking virtually all the glasses and whiskey bottles. "God be with you," she said before she climbed back into her buggy.

Arrested some 30 times, she paid her fines through lecture fees and the sale of souvenir hatchets to temperance advocates.

In Miami, she visited a saloon and an illegal gambling room downtown and then hit North Miami, a community at that time of many saloons, gambling dens and brothels. By this time she was less into smashing things, preferring instead to lecture, lobby and expose what she considered the evils of drinking.

Notorious Banyan Street in West Palm Beach was one place that drew Carry's ire. The town had struggled for years with this problem thoroughfare, also known as Whiskey Street because of its saloons.

President Theodore Roosevelt refused to let Carry visit the White House to harangue him. In typical acerbic style, Mrs. Nation snapped: "All the nations are welcome – except Carry."

Though Carry Nation's great dream, Prohibition, came true in 1918, it was the Roosevelts who had the last laugh. For it was during Franklin Roosevelt's first administration, in 1933, that the hated no-boozing law was finally repealed.

Carrie Nation on Banyan Street, West Palm Beach.
(Historical Society of Palm Beach County)

George Landrum Blount, Pompano Pioneer

As a man who came from humble beginnings, George Landrum Blount could appreciate a fine home.

The son of a circuit-riding Southern Baptist minister in rural Georgia, he had known nights when he went to bed hungry while his father was away preaching. In 1906 he arrived in Pompano, where he went to work as a surveyor for the Florida Coast Line and Transportation Company.

In time, he bought 12 acres from the company, five of them coastal muckland, the rest a drier parcel to the west.

Blount and his brothers, William and Devotie, became successful farmers. They all lived together in a large frame house they built.

After he married Mary Thomas in 1914, George began to think about a separate home for his own family. In 1921, he began constructing a spacious home on a large lot he owned at NE Sixth Street and Fifth Avenue in old Pompano.

The big, two-story, yellow brick house he built became a Pompano landmark. When the killer hurricane of 1926 struck Broward County, people in Pompano knew where to go. Some 30 frightened souls showed up at Blount's house that night, a tribute to its solid construction.

The town's first clerk after its 1908 incorporation, George Blount died in 1959, just short of his eightieth birthday. In time, the old Blount family home passed into other hands.

If he could return and see it now, Blount would react with total amazement. His house has become the Islamic Center of South Florida, and a second building on his

George Blount. *(Fort Lauderdale Historical Society)*

property supports a mid-eastern dome topped with a crescent, a symbol of the Moslem faith.

Would Blount have approved? Maybe. A dedicated teetotaler, he worked for years against the sale of liquor in Pompano – and the religion of Islam prohibits alcohol.

The George Blount home. *(Robert Azmitia, Sunshine Magazine)*

D.W. Griffith Finds a South Seas Paradise

They hit town the last week of November, 1919 – a crew of some 50 actors, actresses, cameramen and technicians, and the legendary director himself.

The Hotel Broward, though not yet completed, hastily flung open its doors to the crew. The director was given the honor of placing the first signature on the hotel's register. He signed it "David Wark Griffith."

D.W. Griffith, America's greatest filmmaker of the silent era, had come to Fort Lauderdale to shoot *Rainbow Isle,* a tale of the South Seas. On the shores of the New River he found the tropical wonderland his film needed.

By this time Griffith was already a legend. He had transformed film into something close to an art form and given the public such movie classics as *The Birth of a Nation, Intolerance* and *Broken Blossoms.*

The film he would make here would hardly qualify as one of the all-time greats, but that was of little concern to the people of Fort Lauderdale. To the townsfolk, this was excitement, this was the big time. They could mingle with such great stars as Richard Barthelmess and the promising starlet, Clarine Seymour.

Most of the city turned out to watch. Many of the town's citizens appeared in bit parts or as extras. Marion Reed, daughter of former mayor, Capt. Will Reed, appeared in the movie, which would finally be named *The Idol Dancer.*

To populate the "island" with natives, Griffith gave jobs to many local blacks and Seminole Indians.

School girls picked up extra money and amused the big-city moviemakers with their small-town modesty.

The girls had no objection to letting the makeup men apply the brown paint that transformed them into dusky South Seas maidens, but insisted on applying all leg makeup themselves.

A native village was built on the grounds of the Las Olas Inn, which at that time boasted a superb grove of coconut palms. Many scenes were shot in the area that would later become Idlewyld, still others on the grounds of Frank Stranahan's home on the river, and the Hugh Taylor Birch estate, now a state park on Sunrise Boulevard.

Tragedy marred the filming, though no one realized it at the time. Clarine Seymour, the leading lady, fell from a coconut tree and suffered internal injuries. She completed the film but died soon afterward in New York from complications from the fall.

When location photography was finished, Griffith was honored by local businessmen at a dinner at the Hotel Broward. In after-dinner remarks, Griffith said:

"You people who live here and pursue your daily occupations amidst the natural tropical beauty of the country, probably do not realize how wonderful your country is. But to one who has never seen it before it is a revelation. There may be a more beautiful river in the world than the New River...but if so I have never seen it."

Unfortunately for filmmakers, Fort Lauderdale's career as a South Seas island was just about over. The Florida land boom would end its age of innocence forever.

D.W. Griffith, seated. *(Fort Lauderdale Historical Society)*

Mr. Brook Sold Lauds for Lauderdale

Not many people had heard of Fort Lauderdale when Auylan Harcourt Brook arrived there in 1919.

An advertising man and a creator of large billboards and neon signs, Brook was the perfect choice for a man to begin polishing the city's image.

In 1921, he shanghaied President-elect Warren G. Harding, who was cruising down the Intracoastal en route to Miami. After blocking Harding's pathway with a large dredge, Brook conveniently appeared with his yacht to rescue the president. For the next two days all newspaper stories about Harding bore the unfamiliar dateline, "Fort Lauderdale, Florida."

The city's first booster had honed his skills in the New York market. As "Mr. Brook from Brooklyn," he was famed for large electrical display signs.

In Fort Lauderdale he painted a huge sign at the Florida East Coast Railway station, inviting passengers to "get off and catch one." He was referring to tarpon. On the Andrews Avenue bridge he installed mounted fish in glass cases to catch the eye of fun-loving visitors.

Brook developed Fort Lauderdale's first advertising campaign, started South Florida's first big game-fishing contest, and became first commodore of the Lauderdale Yacht Club.

When he reached 80, the Commodore danced a jig and cried out, "I've made it!"

Indeed he had. But when he decided to prove he could still stand on his head, he ruptured a blood vessel in his neck. It proved fatal.

Brook billboard that greeted passengers at the Florida East Coast Railway station. *(Fort Lauderdale Historical Society)*

Commodore A.H. Brook. *(Fort Lauderdale Historical Society)*

To honor the man who put Fort Lauderdale on the map, the city named one of the main routes to the beach the Brook Memorial Causeway. Ironically, the name failed to catch on. Today, people call Brook's road the 17th Street Causeway.

The Legend of the Indian in Drag

Back in the 1920s, strange legends attached themselves to the fluttering shirttails of an Indian named Charlie Tommie.

He was a drunkard and a panhandler. He was also a local institution, a colorful figure seen often on the streets of Fort Lauderdale. He was always attired in a strange garment sometimes described as a woman's dress, sometimes as a man's shirt with very long shirttails.

Charlie often begged for money to buy medicine for his feet, the "foot-medicine" being whiskey. On one occasion he asked a man for a quarter because he was sick.

Sick how and where? the man asked. Charlie rubbed his stomach.

"Well, I'm a doctor," the man said, "and I'll fix you up in a jiffy." He promptly prepared a dark liquid in a glass. Charlie drank it tentatively.

"Still, sick," he grunted and walked away.

No one remembers just when people began calling him Shirttail Charlie. Stories were invented and repeated until they became legends. And Charlie offered his own elaborate biography, most of which was untrue.

A popular scenario went like this: Charlie had murdered his wife, was exiled from the tribe and doomed to spend the rest of his life in a woman's dress.

According to this legend, one inch was supposed to have been removed from the hem of Charlie's dress each year. Had he lived long enough, he might have eventually won fame as the local nudist.

But Charlie didn't live that long. Sometime around 1930 he finally drank himself to death. He was found face down in a mud puddle, and was buried near the Seaboard railroad tracks, just north of Broward Boulevard.

What was the truth about Charlie's crime and punishment? Ivy Stranahan, a pioneer and friend of the Seminoles since the late 1890s, cleared up the matter of the so-called "murder."

"Gossip has it that he killed his wife," she wrote. "This is definitely not so. She died of natural causes."

Mrs. Stranahan should know. Her husband, Frank, buried Charlie's wife.

Why then did Charlie wear the dress?

Patsy West, curator of the Seminole/Miccosukee Photo Archives, believes that Charlie wore the dress simply because he was a traditionalist. At a time when many Seminoles had begun to wear the white man's trousers, Charlie stayed with Indian garb, a long colorful dress, or shirt.

West feels that Charlie was not formally banished. Being a drunk was enough to make him an outcast.

Whatever the truth, his legend lives on. Two Fort Lauderdale restaurants have already been named for him. The first operated some years ago near where he was buried. The current Shirttail Charlie's is a popular seafood restaurant on the New River. Charlie would have loved its bar.

Shirttail Charlie skinning an alligator. *(Fort Lauderdale Historical Society)*

A Hispanic Architect in Broward

The most famous of all boomtime South Florida architects, Addison Mizner, designed no houses south of Boca Raton. Nonetheless, Broward County managed to come through the 1920s land rush with a trendy Spanish-style architect all its own.

His name was Francis L. Abreu, and he was born in 1896 in non-Hispanic Newburgh, N.Y., in a house bearing the non-Hispanic name of "Dannskammer."

Abreu's parents, however, were decidedly Hispanic. His mother, Marie, was the daughter of Juan Jacinto Jova, a wealthy Spanish national; his father, Diego Abreu, was a Cuban sugar cane planter educated in Spain. As a boy, Francis divided his time between Dannskammer and Cuba.

In the early '20s the Abreu family was attracted to Fort Lauderdale. Diego lived in a guest house on the ocean and then purchased property at Tarpon Bend. Other members of the Jova clan also became winter residents.

Meanwhile, Francis had graduated from Cornell, where he studied architecture and fine arts.

A young architect just starting out needs a good commission to show what he can do. Unfortunately, most people won't give him one until he has already shown his merit. A classic "Catch-22."

This is where a rich family helps. The Jovas were among Abreu's first clients. Juan Jacinto Jova, his grandfather, asked him to design a beach house at Alhambra Street and A1A. It appears that the project was intended to showcase the young architect's considerable talents, as well as provide his grandparents with a fine oceanside mansion.

The house, still standing, featured many details that continued to surface in his later work, among them a tower entrance way and a large arched window, facing the water.

Abreu went on to design many beautiful Spanish-style homes, a number of them on the New River. Among his other projects were the Wilton Manors Arches, the Dania Beach Hotel, the *Pompano News* Building, the Wahoo Beach Lodge in Pompano Beach, the Maxwell Arcade, the Bryan Court on Southwest Second Street, the Fort Lauderdale Municipal Casino and Pool, and the Fort Lauderdale Golf and Country Club.

After the land "bust" settled over South Florida, Abreu moved to Georgia, where he designed a home on Sea Island for America's premier playwright, Eugene O'Neil.

Abreu's firm became one of the most succesful in Georgia. He died in 1969, but he left behind enough structures to remind people that Hispanic influence is nothing new in South Florida.

Fort Lauderdale Golf and Country Club. *(Fort Lauderdale Historical Society)*

"Pops" in the Venetian Pool

Today, it would be called a "photo opportunity." But in 1925, when Paul Whiteman and his orchestra climbed into the Venetian Pool in Coral Gables, it was business as usual.

In the Roaring Twenties, developers used pop music and big bands to sell real estate all over South Florida. And the buoyant Whiteman had one of the biggest bands going. "Pops" Whiteman was known for his contributions to jazz, and in 1924 had commissioned a young composer to write a serious jazz piece. The result was George Gershwin's *Rhapsody in Blue.* Much later, the dulcet-voiced Bing Crosby would sing with Whiteman's band.

But on that day in 1925, Whiteman, at the behest of Coral Gables developer George Merrick, took his show into the pool. The following year Merrick decided against the water treatment for the new Miami Grand Opera Company. When the company performed its first recital, the 900,000-gallon pool was drained so that the singers and the orchestra could perform for an audience seated at the bottom of an empty pool.

Composers got into the gee-but-it's-great act, too, creating such memorable boomtime songs as *When the Moon Shines in Coral Gables, Coral Gables, I Love You,* *Underneath Miami's Dreamy Moon, Dreams of Fulford-by-the-Sea,* and a strange foxtrot called *Tamiami Trail.*

Well-known songwriters Harry Warren *(Along Miami's Shores)*, Dick Whiting *(While Miami Dreams)*, and Al Jolson *(Florida Moon)*, tried their hands, but it wasn't until the pit of the Depression, 1935, that Joe Burke penned Miami's, most cherished song, *Moon Over Miami.* This became the title – and theme song – of a 1941 movie musical starring Alice Faye and Don Ameche.

Burke's tune is not to be confused with *Miami Moon,* written by songwriter/realtor E. St. Clair Piggott. That song was a hit, too, and for a time Piggott was known locally as "Mr. Moon."

Years later, he continued to combine his two careers, working out of the Moon Real Estate Studio. Prospective homebuyers might wander into his office and find him seated at the piano, singing, *"And when the night of joy is almost over/You drive your car to a place where moonbeams play. Miami moon, dream on, dream on."*

Paul Whiteman and his orchestra in the Venetian Pool, 1925. Whiteman in foreground with baton. *(Historical Association of Southern Florida)*

Bryan on the Stump for Coral Gables

The year was 1925. The place was Coral Gables, and the pitchman was one of America's greatest orators – William Jennings Bryan.

Three times, Bryan's silver tongue had gained him the Democratic Party's nomination for president. But while he could stir the crowds with his passionate oratory, Bryan had failed to win the nation's highest office. However, he did serve as secretary of state in Woodrow Wilson's administration.

Several years later, one of the lesser-known chapters in Bryan's career found him using his eloquence to hype the virtues of South Florida real estate.

When George Merrick was developing Coral Gables into the City Beautiful, he always sought the services of the best. And he knew that, in the world of speechmaking, Bryan had no equal.

To make matters easier, Bryan was already living in Miami and was a fervent believer in his adopted state. He had first come to Florida 25 years earlier for the inauguration of his cousin, W.S. Jennings, as governor. Later, Bryan and his wife moved to Miami and lived in their famous bayfront home Villa Serena.

So, at the height of the Florida land boom, Bryan was hired to stroll out onto a platform in the middle of Coral Gables' spectacular Venetian Pool and tell a group of would-be buyers of the wonders of Coral Gables, the glories of South Florida's weather and of the fabulous benefits that real estate investment could bring.

Merrick paid Bryan $100,000 a year, half in cash, half in land. Bryan invested some of the money in Broward County real estate, buying six large lots in Richlands, a subdivision west of Fort Lauderdale.

In the midst of the mad frenzy of the Florida land boom, Bryan also found time to teach a Bible class in Miami's Royal Palm Park. By 1925, his eighth year with the class, he could proudly point to 8,000 members. It was America's largest Sunday school class, an island of serenity surrounded by America's biggest real estate binge.

A lawyer and newspaper editor from Platte, Nebraska, Bryan burst into lasting fame in 1896 when he delivered one of the most famous orations in American history. As a delegate to the National Democratic Convention that year, he concluded a dramatic speech against the gold standard with the ringing words, "You shall not press down upon the brow of labor this crown of thorns, you shall not crucify mankind upon a cross of gold!"

The speech electrified the convention. Bryan, who had come as an unknown 36-year-old delegate, walked away with the nomination.

Later in 1925, the year the land boom reached its peak, Bryan left Miami to assist the prosecution in the famous "monkey trial" in Dayton, Tennessee. A schoolteacher named John Scopes had been arrested for teachings

William Jennings Bryan at the Venetian Pool, Coral Gables. (*Historical Association of Southern Florida*)

based on the theory of evolution, contrary to state law. The attorney for the defense was the legendary Clarence Darrow.

Bryan, arguing for the literal interpretation of the Bible, won the case, but he never left Dayton alive. An advocate of temperance in regard to alcohol, Bryan ate too much lunch on a scorching July day and died from over-eating – an ignominious end to an extraordinary career.

That Magnificent Flier Named Fogg

Fort Lauderdale's first airport was named for a dashing dare-devil who brought aviation to Broward County in the Roaring Twenties.

His name was Merle Fogg. Unfortunately, this meant that the airport was called Fogg Field, an unhappy combination of words for fliers. Today a much expanded version is called Fort Lauderdale-Hollywood International Airport.

The first licensed aviator in his native state of Maine, Fogg came to Fort Lauderdale in 1925 to pilot a seaplane bought by one of the city's most prominent businessmen, Tom Bryan.

Fogg built a runway and a hangar and set up the Merle Fogg Flying Service on the south side of Las Olas Boulevard near the Intracoastal Waterway. He taught flying, flew sightseeing trips and put on aerial shows. He flew the first land plane from Florida to Nassau, flew friends to Miami for hamburgers, and took off over the Everglades to drop urgent messages to hunting parties. The story goes that he once lassoed a deer from his biplane while flying over the Glades, although exactly how he did it isn't clear.

After the 1926 hurricane devastated Broward, Fogg offered his services for emergency and relief work. He flew August Burghard, a reporter for the *Fort Lauderdale Daily News,* over the stricken area to gather facts for his hurricane story.

Fogg and Burghard were close friends, roommates in fact. Burghard had selected Merle to be best man at his wedding, which was set for June, 1928, in Macon, Georgia. Merle Fogg never made it. He was killed in a plane crash at a West Palm Beach orange grove. A student pilot was at the controls.

Fogg's death came on May Day, 1928. Exactly one year later, the Merle Fogg Airport was dedicated. It was built on the site of the city's former municipal golf course.

At the dedication, a monument was unveiled, a plaque set in a block of Maine granite. When the Navy expanded Fogg Field in World War II, the monument to Fogg was shoved aside and was lost sight of for 30 years.

When it was rediscovered, the Daughters of the American Revolution had it moved to a small city park on Las Olas Boulevard – just a short distance from the site where Fogg had established his flying service more than a half-century earlier.

Merle Fogg and biplane, ca. 1926. *(Fort Lauderdale Historical Society)*

Barron of Wall Street

Clarence W. Barron looked like the publisher of *The Wall Street Journal* ought to look, every inch and every pound the classic "fat cat."

Usually carrying 300 pounds on a 5-foot, 6-inch frame, Barron maintained a wardrobe in six progressively larger sizes. When he could wear only the largest, he knew he was 50 pounds above his preferred weight of 300. It was time, then, to head for Dr. Kellogs's sanitorium in Battle Creek, Mich., to shape up.

Barron was a familiar figure in Miami during the mid-1920s, when the Florida real estate boom became one of the world's most important business stories. Instead of wearing waist coats and silk ties, as he did at his office in New York, he wisely switched to an all-white ensemble complete with a white straw hat.

In a February 1925 *Journal* story datelined "Somewhere on Bay Biscayne," Barron reported on the enormous growth of Miami: "Side streets are filled, traffic on the main highway is slower than in New York City, and traffic cops have more work than in any city in the North."

The motor car helped fuel the boom, Barron observed, because it had made South Florida accessible to so many people. The traffic jams were nothing to rival today's gridlocks on I-95, but Barron saw the birth of what would become an ever-present problem: "10,000 motors, too many to handle."

As a young man, Barron founded business news bureaus in Boston and Philadelphia and was enlisted by Charles Dow and Edward Jones to serve as the Boston correspondent for their *Wall Street Journal*.

In 1901, at 46, he purchased Dow Jones. Over the next 27 years, he expanded the *Journal* into the nation's most widely read daily newspaper. In 1921 he founded *Barron's* a financial weekly newspaper.

Despite his weight, Barron, it was said, did the work of six men. Three secretaries accompanied him on his trips to Europe. Once in Paris he took all three with him to the *Folies Bergere* and dictated to them during the performance. Said writer Lucius Beebee: "The management was torn between admiration and outrage."

He worked hard until he died at 73 of pneumonia. His last words were, "What's the news?"

Clarence W. Barron, strolling outside Miami's Royal Palm Hotel in 1927. *(Romer Collection, Miami-Dade Public Library)*

"Doc" Sistrunk's 5,000 Babies

During his 44 years in Fort Lauderdale, Dr. James Franklin Sistrunk brought an estimated 5,000 babies into the world. Recalls one 40-year resident:

"Doc Sistrunk always knew his babies, too. No matter how old they were, he could point at them and say, 'That is one of mine.'"

Although a Dr. Henry H. Green practiced medicine in Fort Lauderdale briefly before moving on to Miami, Dr. Sistrunk is regarded today as Broward County's first black physician – and for 16 years its only one.

He was born in Midway, Florida, just west of Tallahassee, in 1891. After serving in World War I, he completed his education in 1919, graduating from Meharry College in Nashville, Tennessee. After practicing briefly in Dunnellon, he moved to Fort Lauderdale and continued his practice until shortly before his death in 1966 at the age of 75.

Before Dr. Sistrunk's arrival, Broward's growing black population was dependent on white doctors for medical treatment, and even after he opened his office on Metcalf (now Northwest Fifth Avenue), Sistrunk was somewhat restricted in the medical services he could provide. In those days, blacks were not permitted to perform surgery in white hospitals.

In 1938, Sistrunk was joined by Dr. Von D. Mizell. Together they established Provident Hospital, the city's first medical facility for blacks. Dr. Sistrunk became chief of staff. Later he also served on the staff at Broward General Hospital.

Staff of Fort Lauderdale's Provident Hospital, 1946. Dr. Sistrunk, second from right, and Dr. Von D. Mizell, third from left, founded the hospital. *(Fort Lauderdale Historical Society)*

Dr. James Franklin Sistrunk. *(Fort Lauderdale Historical Society)*

Sistrunk's greatest contribution to Broward County, however, came not through the hospital he helped to start, but through his long years as a classic "country doctor," a kindly, white-haired healer of the sick, an easygoing man who made house calls and forgot the bills if a patient had no money.

Today, his name is commemorated all over Fort Lauderdale – in Sistrunk Boulevard, in the J.F. Sistrunk Bridge over the north fork of the New River, and in the J.F. Sistrunk Children's Pavilion, the pediatrics ward at the hospital he helped to found.

But to the people who knew him, he'll always be remembered simply as "Doc" Sistrunk.

The "Liberace" of the Violin

At a hotel in Washington, D.C., he once registered as "Rubinoff and his Violin." They were an inseparable pair.

David Rubinoff was solo violinist and orchestra leader on the *Chase & Sanborn Hour* with Eddie Cantor, the most popular radio show in America from 1932 to 1934. At his peak, Rubinoff played more concerts than any other musician in the country, averaging 300 a year.

His showmanship drew crowds that would make today's rock stars envious. Once, in Chicago's Grant Park, 225,000 people attended an open-air Rubinoff concert.

Among Rubinoff's many fans was a Miami cabinet maker named Charles Roman. Born in Hungary in 1893, Roman came to Miami in 1917. Years later he declared, "I am now a cracker."

A master craftsman, Roman formed the Royal Palm Furniture Co. He specialized in building humidity-resistant, solid-wood furniture, carved from native woods – oak, gum, ash and magnolia.

It was Roman's hobby, however, that brought him to Rubinoff. Understandably, for a native of Hungary, he loved the violin. In fact, he made more than a hundred of them.

Rubinoff owned a Roman violin and delighted the cabinet maker by playing it on occasion when he performed in Miami.

Most of the time, however, Rubinoff's violin was his 200-year-old Stradivarius, insured for $100,000.

Rubinoff was born in Grodno, Russia, in 1897. At age five he was playing the balalaika so well that the town's music master gave him free lessons. His parents, who had wanted him to be a barber, invested three dollars in a violin. A scholarship to the Warsaw Conservatory then launched him on his musical career. When he was 15, his family moved to Pittsburgh.

Rubinoff's big break came on Eddie Cantor's show. Cantor recalled him fondly:

"He was one of the great showmen of the business – a good violinist rather than a great violinist, but a showman who gave the impression of being all the great violinists put together. He was a ham, publicity conscious, publicity wise and publicity wild."

Rubinoff even published a newspaper about himself.

Said violin-maker Charles Roman: "He was the Liberace of 1940."

Violinist David Rubinoff, right, visits with Charles Roman and his wife. *(Romer Collection, Miami-Dade Public Library)*

Harry's Little Piece of Heaven

Some would say Harry S. Truman made Key West richer just by drawing world attention to the island city during his 11 working vacations there as president. More tourists, more dollars.

On March 12, 1949, Truman directly made a lot of Key West numbers players richer — and a few "bolita" houses a good deal poorer.

In the arcane world of numbers wagering (known in Spanish as bolita), "45" stands for president. And since Truman was greeted with the traditional 21-gun salute, numbers players all over the island bought the 21-45 combination. It hit, at odds of 80 to 1.

No wonder they loved him in Key West. One of the city's main streets, Truman Avenue, is named after him. His daughter is remembered through the Margaret Truman Launderette.

Harry Truman made Key West the Little White House in the late fall of 1946, partly because the submarine base there had ample accommodations, already located on secure government property, and partly because he needed warmer weather to shake a lingering cold. On November 18 he wrote his mother:

"I left Washington yesterday morning in a rain and a fog with the temperature at 40 degrees. Arrived here at three p.m. in sunshine and 80 degrees. They put me up in a Southern-built house with galleries all around, upstairs and down...I've just returned from the beach...and my cough and cold are nearly gone already."

During another visit in 1948, on November 11, he wrote his sister, pointing out that Armistice Day was particularly special for him, dating back to his service in World War I:

"I am on my way to the beach to take a swim. Just 30 years ago I was firing a final barrage at the heinies at a little town...northeast of Verdun. Some change of position, I'd say."

The relaxing spell of Key West engulfed the president. Once he unexpectedly called a press conference. Reporters anticipating an earth-shaking announcement saw the president walk in wearing a loud tropical shirt and a pith helmet.

It turned out to be a reverse press conference, with Truman asking all the question: How late were they out last night? Had they had breakfast? Had they written their wives in the past week?

One of the biggest laughs for Harry Truman, wife Bess and daughter Margaret came when a 1950 census taker showed up at the Little White House. She asked the president what his occupation was.

President Truman in Key West, late 1940s. (*Monroe County Public Library*)

We Loved Them, Yeah, Yeah, Yeah

Do you think anyone will be in Miami to meet us?" Paul McCartney asked stewardess Carol Gallagher. On their first trip to America, four working-class lads from Liverpool, England, better known as the Beatles, were approaching Miami International Airport on National Airlines Flight II, fresh from triumphs in New York on the *Ed Sullivan Show* and at Carnegie Hall.

As it turned out, Miami produced the largest airport crowd of the Beatles' 1964 tour. More than 10,000 screaming South Florida fans, mostly teenagers, surged against the outmanned police, straining for a glimpse of the Fab Four – McCartney, George Harrison, John Lennon and Ringo Starr. They stampeded their way through police barricades, smashed windows and broke down doors. The scene was described as "near extermination."

The young musicians escaped physical harm as limousines whisked them away, across Biscayne Bay to the Deauville Hotel on Miami Beach. It would be their home while in South Florida and the scene of another performance on Sullivan's popular Sunday night television show.

When they arrived in Miami, the phenomenon called Beatlemania was less than a year old. The riotous welcomes, the screaming, the uncontrollable enthusiasm had started in England the previous May.

Still, in February of 1964, the Beatles were not quite the household name they would later become. At the beach, Paul met a 17-year-old Miami Beach High School senior to whom he took a liking. When he telephoned Diane Levine, her father asked, "Who's this guy Paul McCartney calling you?"

Buddy Dresner, a North Miami Beach policeman, was put in charge of the Beatles' security. He did more than

The Beatles at the Deauville Hotel. *(Historical Association of Southern Florida)*

that. He taught them how to fish, took them to their first drive-in movie, introduced them to their first grilled cheese sandwiches.

The Dresners invited the Liverpool lads to their home for a homecooked meal of roast beef, potatoes, string beans and strawberry shortcake. Buddy's wife, Dottie, was delighted. "Ringo cut my son's potato," she said.

Dresner liked to kid the Beatles: "You guys better save your money. I don't think you're going to make it."

The number of tickets issued to the Sunday night show was greater than the number of seats at the Deauville's Napoleon Room. The result: misery.

Many kids, standing in long lines, were turned away. Some, from the University of Miami, joined forces with a group from Detroit that had flown to Miami to continue its "Stamp out the Beatles" campaign. McCartney in turn called for a Beatles' counterattack to "Stamp out Detroit."

Police moved in to stop the clashes between pro- and anti-Beatle factions. Inside, it was even wilder.

Eddie Liles, who ran the Deauville, told *Rolling Stone* magazine: "On the night the Beatles appeared on the *Sullivan Show*, I strolled through the theater to see a sight I had never seen before: 5,000 people jammed in the Napoleon Room — screaming, weeping and fainting at the sight of the Beatles. The excitement and electricity generated in the Napoleon Room that night was indescribable. Only Judy Garland's famous comeback in that same room came close to the Beatles' Sullivan appearance.

An unidentified fan presents Florida souvenirs to the Beatles. *(Historical Association of Southern Florida)*

"They seemed terribly frightened of the huge crowds. Paul was shy, but he was my favorite. I did everything I could to make him feel at home in America. I even promised him a nice Jewish girl."

A writer reviewing the performance for *The Miami News* delivered a particularly interesting judgment on the four lads who shook the world:

"Their music is passable, the lyrics border on the inane, and the voices are indistinguishable from the hundreds of other groups who subject the human ear to organized cacophany." (History, of course, recorded otherwise.)

On their tour, the Beatles learned to like American clothes. Before they left Miami, Eddie Liles took them shopping at a men's store where they bought $6,295 worth of duds. They charged them to their hotel account. Eight months later the Deauville had to sue to get them to pay their hotel bill.

Said Liles: "I still love the Beatles."

Before leaving Florida the Beatles took time out to overwhelm Key West. At the Key Wester, their entourage occupied all 12 villas across the front of the motel.

One Key West old-timer recalls: "They were even buying water from the pool the Beatles swam in."

Beatlemania was on a rampage, and it hasn't subsided since.

PART SIX

Scoundrels, Scandals and Scams

The Carpetbagger, the Pig, and Dirty Politics

When carpetbagger William H. Gleason of New York State arrived in South Florida in 1866, only a handful of people were living in Dade County – even though in those days it stretched from the Upper Keys to what is now Palm Beach.

For the crafty Gleason, Dade provided a base to launch a political career that saw him elected Florida's first Republican lieutenant governor.

But Gleason had bigger dreams. He seized the state seal, declared himself governor, and set about trying to impeach the duly elected governor.

Creative though the scheme was, it failed. Gleason was himself impeached and kicked out of office.

Still, he had a strong power base in Dade, where among other things he served as self-appointed school board member, even though the county had no schools. He ran the post office and owned the mailboat, modestly named the *Gov. Gleason*.

In 1872 he decided to return to Tallahassee, as Dade's state representative, an easy enough matter to rig since he controlled the county's elective machinery.

Badly needing a candidate to oppose him, the Democrats nominated one John J. "Pig" Brown, a hermit who raised hogs on the New River. "Pig" was the only white resident of the area that later became Fort Lauderdale. He had no way of rejecting the nomination, since his party didn't bother to tell him he had been picked.

When the votes came in, Pig Brown had won, 16-14. Unruffled, Gleason had a henchman invalidate three Brown votes, giving him a 14-13 edge.

Four years later, the two political foes clashed again. Once again Brown outpolled Gleason, 27-24. And once again Gleason challenged the results, citing irregularities at a polling place on property he owned. When the contested votes were thrown out, Gleason won again, 7-4.

This time, however, an indignant legislature refused to seat Gleason. Pig Brown was declared the winner.

Unfortunately, Representative Brown took an unusual view of his duties as an elected official. He sold all his hogs, headed for Tallahassee – and never came back.

William H. Gleason, ca. 1870. *(Historical Association of Southern Florida)*

Life Was Cheap in the Ten Thousand Islands

What remains of the old Watson Place in the Ten Thousand Islands gives little inkling of its bloody, lawless past or the many murders that legend says were committed there. Today, it is just a clearing in the Everglades National Park where boaters on the Wilderness Waterway can camp for the night or break for a picnic.

At the turn of the century, however, the Ten Thousand Islands, a bewildering maze of mangroves, gave cover to fugitives, derelicts and a few harmless hermits. The seven unwritten laws of that wild country, an early account says, were:

1. Suspect every man.
2. Ask no questions.
3. Settle your own quarrels.
4. Never steal from an Islander.
5. Stick by him, even if you do not know him.
6. Shoot quick, when your secret is in danger.
7. Cover your kill.

It was into this last frontier that Ed Watson ventured sometime after 1900. He was a friendly enough man but he was noted, too, for a terrible temper. Rumor had it that he had killed the infamous woman outlaw, Belle Starr, back in the Wild West. True or not, the rumor established Watson as a man to be wary of.

Watson took up farming on the Chatham River, about 10 miles south of Chokoloskee Island on the Gulf Coast. He raised sugar cane, papayas and beans and sold his produce in Key West and Fort Myers.

The newcomer prospered and in time built a dock, a barn and a two-story house. In a land of lean-tos, Watson presented the image of a successful farmer.

Some said he owed his success to cheap labor. In fact, it was suspected he didn't pay his help at all. Most of his workers were fugitives or down-and-outs with no family ties. They worked for Watson, then turned up missing. Many thought they were terminated on payday, but in keeping with the code of the region, nobody asked any questions.

Then, after a brawl in Fort Myers, three men went to Chatham Bend to "get" Watson. A shootout followed. Nobody was killed but one of the men had half of his mustache shot off. People began to call Watson the "Barber" – but not to his face.

Living with Watson at Chatham Bend in the fall of 1910 were five people, among them a large woman named Hannah Smith who was known as Big Six, a man named Leslie Cox and an old black man whose name was not known. In October of that year, a group of Chokoloskee clam-diggers discovered the body of Big Six near Watson's place.

Soon afterwards, the old black man turned up in Chokoloskee with confused tales of murders at Chatham Bend. Watson arrived next. He admitted there had been murders but said that Cox had committed them.

The Ed Watson place in the Ten Thousand Islands. (*Historical Association of Southern Florida*)

The people on Chokoloskee wanted the sheriff to investigate. But the sheriff didn't want to go to Chatham Bend. A hurricane in October, 1910, may have altered the sheriff's plans. It certainly affected Watson's future. Watson set off to hunt for Cox with storm-wet shotgun shells.

Later that month, Watson arrived again in Chokoloskee, carrying a shotgun in one hand and a pistol on his hip. Unfortunately for him, most of the crowd that greeted him also carried guns.

Watson told the crowd that he had killed Cox, and for proof produced a hat he said belonged to Cox. The crowd was unconvinced, although some of the men agreed to return to Chatham Bend to see the body. Someone raised the question of whether Watson should be allowed to carry his gun. An argument followed and Watson pulled both the shotgun's triggers. The gun, loaded with wet shells, misfired. At that point, practically the whole crowd blazed away at Watson. So many bullets pierced his body that no one knew who really killed him. And no one tried very hard to find out.

Whether Watson had really killed Cox, or which if either of them killed Big Six, remains a mystery to this day. Cox, for his part, was never heard from again.

Selling Lots of Soggy Lots

Monster land development schemes seem to come with the territory in South Florida. But few have threatened to overwhelm Fort Lauderdale like the one dreamed up by Richard J. "Dicky" Bolles in 1911.

In a two-week period he lured more than 3,000 people into a town which then had a resident population of less than 150. Bolles had a half-million acres of Everglades land to sell. He had bought it from the state for one million dollars. Most of it was downright soggy.

To sell the land, Bolles, a New Yorker who had made a fortune in Colorado gold mines, came up with an elaborate promotion. His Florida Fruit Lands Company introduced the contract method of land sales, which he tied in with a lottery so skillfully disguised as an auction that it was just barely legal.

Bolles' idea was to separate prospective landowners from $240 for a contract entitling them to own a lot in Progresso, just north of what was then Fort Lauderdale, and a farm in the Everglades. The size and location of the farm would depend on the luck of the draw in a lottery carefully rigged to look like an auction. It was pre-arranged that each buyer, when his number was called, would bid exactly $240 and that no one would bid against him.

Bolles' "swamp-boomers" toured the Midwest, motivating farmers with descriptions of the Everglades as a "tropical paradise," "promised land," "land of destiny" and the "magnet whose climate and agriculture would bring the human flood."

Trainload after trainload showed up in March, 1911, until over 3,000 of them had been shoe-horned into the little community. Most of them stayed in tents. The big event had the town bulging but at the same time it provided jobs. The three hotels needed extra chefs, bellboys and clerks. Townspeople became real estate salesmen and the Fort Lauderdale *Weekly Herald* became the *Daily Herald* for four days before expiring.

After the binge was over, buyers became aware that much of their land was under water. Bolles and his top aides were indicted by the federal government on 22 counts, covering a wide variety of charges. Even the Fort Lauderdale town attorney, J.L. Billingsley, was arrested.

Bolles' defense was based on a claim of good faith, arising from the state's promises that it would convert the Glades into fertile farmland. The charges were dropped.

Ironically, most of the Glades farmland turned out to be worthless, while the in-town Progresso lots, thrown in as a sales gimmick, proved to be good investments. Progresso, basically, was the area near Andrews Avenue between what is now Sixth Street and Sunrise Boulevard.

Today, Progresso lives on in name only, as Progresso Drive and a small shopping center called Progresso Plaza.

"Dicky" Bolles, third from right, with land lottery aides. *(Fort Lauderdale Historical Society)*

The Scam on New River

In the early 1920s, law enforcers started tapping telephone lines for the first time, to trap bootleggers. Not long afterwards, a gang of well-dressed, middle-aged Fort Lauderdale scam artists also began using wiretapping – to fleece greedy tourists.

Headquarters for the group was the Frank Oliver house on the New River. The wiretappers drove high-powered cars, joined the local golf club, tipped well, and paid their rent on time.

They put up a good front, but inside the house, from which local residents were excluded, a fake bookie operation was under way. It was as elaborate in its planning and execution as the bookie scam immortalized in the Paul Newman-Robert Redford movie, *The Sting.*

The gang leader's gorgeous girlfriend helped lure out-of-towners inside, where they were told that tapped wires provided racing results before the other horse parlors. Thus, a bet could be placed at another parlor on a race in which the winner was already known.

The "mark" would win his first bet, then be persuaded to send home for a large sum of money for another sure-thing bet. When he won this time, he would be told that to collect his huge winnings he would have to go to the syndicate's headquarters in New Orleans. On the train there, his wiretapper companion, who would of course be carrying the money for the phony bet, would simply slip away.

Few questioned why, if the wiretappers could win at will, they didn't just place their own bets. Since the victim was betting illegally, he was reluctant to go to the police. But in time, word of what was going on got around, and law-abiding citizens called for action. However, the sheriff, A.W. Turner, just looked the other way.

The locals then appealed to Florida Governor Cary Hardee. The governor sent a special investigator, Bob Shackleford, down from Jacksonville, who deputized citizens for a raid.

Shackleford's men struck on February 19, 1922. All but two of the so-called wiretappers were captured, along with $7,000 in cash, which was found lying on a table covered with green cloth.

The scam artists, most of them New Yorkers, easily posted bail of $18,000. They seemed confident that no dire actions would be taken against them.

They were right. They didn't even have to show up at their trial. Instead, their lawyer pleaded them guilty, and their fines just happened to total the exact amount of their bail money: $18,000.

Although no official records substantiate the story, it was common talk in Fort Lauderdale that the men were let go without prison sentences as part of a deal in which a particular sum of money would be earmarked for the

The Frank Oliver House in the 1950's. *(Fort Lauderdale Historical Society)*

construction of the county's first hospital, the Edwards-Maxwell Hospital on East Broward Boulevard. That sum of money? You guessed it: $18,000.

In 1923, the state legislature passed an act allowing Broward to issue bonds for the hospital in an amount not to exceed $18,000.

And what became of the house used by the scam artists? It survived into the 1950s, and was later demolished to make room for the expansion of the present *News/Sun-Sentinel* building.

Wilson, the "Other" Mizner

It seems quite fashionable these days to talk about, to hold seminars about and even to write books about architect Addison Mizner, who gave Palm Beach its "look" and then started Boca Raton on its path to fame.

But who knows the story of an even more incredible Mizner – Addison's scoundrel of a younger brother, the late, great Wilson Mizner, a man who once remarked, "Why, if I ever start to tell the story of my life, it will be interrupted by the blowing of a million police whistles"?

Maybe he exaggerated, but the Peck's Bad Boy of the Mizner clan spent much of his life moving back and forth across the thin line that divides the lawful from the unlawful.

Born in 1876, Wilson was the descendant of an old and prominent Northern California family. He grew to become a widely traveled con man, gambler and sports promoter.

He ran a badger game in Alaska in Gold Rush days, oversaw illegal gambling joints around the country, and engaged in cardsharping on luxury liners. He briefly, and unsuccessfully, ran a banana plantation in Guatemala, where his father had once set up his headquarters while serving as U.S. ambassador to five Central American countries.

Wilson's greatest legacy may turn out to be the memorable one-liners his wise-cracking, irreverent tongue cast forth, among them:

"The first hundred years are the hardest." And, "If you copy from one author, it's plagiarism. If you copy from two, it's research." And this piece of sage advice: "Be nice to people on the way up because you'll meet them on the way down."

Wilson tried his hand at managing prizefighters, starting with a trained bear in the Rocky Mountains and then working his way up to one of boxing's greatest, middle-weight champion Stanley Ketchel.

With that kind of background, it was inevitable that he would eventually wind up in Florida. Actually, Addison brought his brother to Palm Beach in 1924, not because he really needed Wilson as an executive assistant but to try to cure him of morphine addiction.

Wilson became secretary-treasurer of the Mizner Corporation, putting many of his shiftless ways behind him as he worked hard to make a success of the varied Mizner projects.

The pair was joined by publicist Harry Reichenbach, whose slogan was, "Get the big snobs and the little snobs will follow." During the peak of the 1924-25 boom, sales at the Mizners' firm averaged two million dollars a week.

A born con man's tendency to overstate finally brought Wilson into conflict with one of the Boca Raton venture's chief financiers, Gen. Coleman Du Pont. Too much razzle-dazzle irked the general, who brought the disagreements out into the open. The juicy publicity that resulted did its bit in bursting the real estate bubble in South Florida. The days of Mizner glory came to an abrupt end.

Undismayed, Wilson went to Hollywood as a screenwriter. After the death of Addison in early 1933, Wilson suffered a severe heart attack in mid-March. Just before he died on April 3, he rejected a clergyman's offer of spiritual consolation, with characteristic wit.

"Much obliged, padre, much obliged," he mumbled as he slipped in and out of a coma. "But why bother? I'll be seeing your boss in a few minutes. I don't expect too much. You can't be a rascal for 40 years and then cop a plea the last minute. God keeps better books than that."

Wilson Mizner. *(Historical Society of Palm Beach County)*

The Day They Wiped Out the Ashley Gang

Today an office supply store stands at the intersection of First Street and First Avenue in Old Pompano, giving slight hint of the armed bank robbery that took place there 60 years ago, a holdup which triggered the downfall of South Florida's most infamous band of outlaws, the Ashley Gang.

The Ashley Gang, composed of Joe Ashley and his five sons, blazed their way into the '20s, commiting bank robberies, murders, hijackings and a continuing string of jail breaks. They were also moonshiners and rum-runners of the first order. They struck from a hideout in the Everglades, and often vanished into the backcountry.

The Ashley family came to southeast Florida when the Florida East Coast Railway was being built. When work on the railroad ran out, the family switched to crime, enlarging the gang from time to time by adding other relatives or friendly lawbreakers.

By 1924, John Ashley, the ringleader, was the only one of the Ashleys still active in the gang. Joe and three of his sons were gunned down along the way. The fourth brother went partly straight, limiting his illicit activities to the relatively genteel business of moonshining.

On September 12, 1924, Joe Tracey, a member of the Ashley Gang, stopped a taxi in West Palm Beach and told the driver, a young man named Wesley Powell, to take him to Deerfield Beach. Along the way, John and two other gang members joined Tracey, tied Powell to a tree and commandeered his cab. Just before closing time the four gangsters slipped into the Bank of Pompano. Cashier Cecil Cates and teller T.H. Myers suddenly found themselves staring down the barrels of unfriendly guns.

The Ashley Gang took $4,000 in cash and a $5,000 bond. It was a good haul for the times, but it proved to be their last. Tired of the Ashley brand of terrorism, lawmen and citizens' posses mobilized to ferret out the gang.

The Bank of Pompano. *(Pompano Beach Library)*

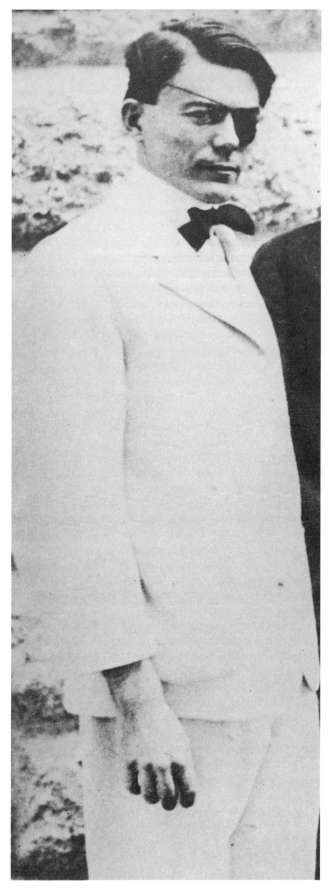

On November 1, an informant told Sheriff Bob Baker of Palm Beach County that the gang would be passing through Fort Pierce that night via the Dixie Highway. At the bridge over Sebastian Inlet, just above Vero Beach, the St. Lucie County sheriff placed a chain barricade.

When they stopped for the chain, the gangsters were quickly surrounded and handcuffed. What happened next is unclear. One account says that Ashley attempted to make a run for it. The certainty is that John Ashley and his three gang members were gunned down.

In those days, lawmen shooting prisoners in handcuffs brought no serious outcries about civil right violations. Most South Floridians were just glad that the Ashleys were finally out of business.

There were a couple of exceptions: Ma Ashley and John's moll, Laura Upthegrove, whose bloodcurdling threats helped persuade Sheriff Baker that it could be hazardous to his health if he made good on his boast to wear John Ashley's glass eye as a watch fob. At the funeral, Ma Ashley, the woman whose husband and sons had terrorized they state for a decade, moaned, "They killed them for not a thing in the world."

John Ashley. *(Fort Lauderdale Historical Society)*

Scamp in Indian Country

People generally liked Egbert L. "Bert" Lasher, a man with a ready smile, a good line of talk and an engaging manner. Unfortunately, Bert Lasher was also a man who all too often moved across the line that divides the lawful from the unlawful. He was, variously, a butcher, a film actor, an actor's agent, a fence, an operator of tourist attractions, a dealer in illegal egret plumes and, finally, the proprietor of a bait-and-tackle shop.

Lasher began to attract notice in the Fort Lauderdale press as early as 1919, when a film crew from Famous Players (later renamed Paramount) came to town to shoot scenes for *The Firing Line.* Based on a famous novel by Robert W. Chambers, the movie starred Irene Castle. Lasher was hired to play the role of a hunting guide in scenes shot near today's Wilton Manors. As an effective actor's agent, he also found work in the movie for two of his hunting dogs, Joe and Prince.

Not long afterward, Lasher served a stint at Raiford prison for dealing in stolen cars. Next he moved on to Miami where he managed somehow to take over as manager of Musa Isle, a tourist attraction that featured (many would say exploited) Seminole Indians in such activities as alligator wrestling.

In gaining the post at Musa Isle, Lasher had to thrust aside a Seminole named Willie Willie by means that many considered less than ethical. Lasher had gotten himself a good job. But he had also gained an enemy.

Lasher stayed at Musa Isle until 1932, when he tried unsuccessfully to make his fortune in New Jersey. He returned to Miami to manage Osceola Gardens, a Seminole attraction at Frenchy's Rendezvous, but this venture went into receivership following a disastrous fire. Later, he wound up out on the Tamiami Trail as proprietor of a bait-and-tackle shop.

But it was as the head man at Musa Isle that he became best known, deferred to as a spokesman for the Indians and something of an authority on the Seminoles.

In 1926, one of Lasher's illegal ventures caught up with him. Through his close ties with the Seminoles, he was actively purchasing illegal egret plumes, which were still being used to decorate women's hats.

Another person who had close ties with the Seminoles at that time was Mrs. Ivy Stranahan, "first lady" of Fort Lauderdale and a long-time friend of the Indians. She was also an active member of the National Audubon Society, which had been the major force in fighting the illegal plume trade.

From her contacts in the tribe she got a tip which she passed on to federal authorities. The result was a raid on Musa Isle.

The anonymous informant who contacted Mrs. Stranahan was believed to be none other than Willie Willie. If so, he enjoyed an impressive revenge. Lasher was convicted in federal court, fined $750 and, worst of all for him, forced to relinquish his claim to a cache of egret plumes valued at $35,000.

No one knows for sure where Bert Lasher ended up, but friends say he began drinking heavily, and died at his bait shop on the Trail sometime in the 1940s, ending a colorful, controversial career.

Bert Lasher in 1927. *(Patsy West, Fort Lauderdale Historical Society)*

Scarface: The Man Florida Didn't Want

South Florida usually welcomes the rich, famous and powerful. Such was not the case with Al "Scarface" Capone.

Shortly after his 1930 release from a Philadelphia penitentiary, the Chicago mobster bought a waterfront estate on Palm Island in Miami Beach. Originally built for St. Louis brewer Clarence Busch, the winter home was purchased for $40,000 – $2,000 down, the rest payable in four annual payments. The interest rate was 8 percent.

Capone took the train to Hollywood where he was met by three bullet-proof automobiles. He rode in the second car, slipping quietly into his home on an Easter Sunday while 40,000 Miamians were in church.

Miami's reaction was instant and angry. The *Miami News* attacked Scarface for moving to the Magic City, and for his tasteless timing. City officials announced that the police would arrest him on sight. The city commission passed a new vagrancy ordinance to make it easier to harass him.

The American Legion even came up with an elaborate scheme to stage a riot. The idea was to force a declaration of martial law, under which constitutional rights could be suspended and Big Al bounced unceremoniously out of town. The plan collapsed when the governor refused to send in the militia.

Of course, opposition was nothing new to Al Capone. Born in Naples, Italy, and raised in New York, he had fought his way to the top of the Chicago mob over the bodies of his rivals. He masterminded gangland's most famous blood-letting, the St. Valentine's Day Massacre.

In true gangland fashion, Capone turned his Florida island home into a fortress. A wall of concrete blocks went up all around the estate and the entrance gate was reinforced with heavy oaken portals.

Capone's move to South Florida made it the "in" place for gang leaders, but he wasn't allowed to enjoy the sunshine for very long. In 1931, a Chicago jury convicted him of income tax evasion. After almost eight years in prison, he retired to Miami, where he died of syphilis.

During the summer of 1930, Capone had flirted with building a palatial home on an isolated peninsula jutting out from Boca Raton into the Hillsboro Canal. He took an option on 50 acres, but dropped his plan after the Boca Raton city fathers gave him a hard time.

In 1952, the Army Corps of Engineers cut a canal through the peninsula, thus separating the property from Boca Raton and creating a Broward County island.

People started calling it Capone Island. Then, in 1977, the island became a county park. The final indignity for Al Capone, the man Florida didn't want, came when the island's name was changed to the bland designation "Deerfield Island Park."

Capone fishing from a cabin cruiser he kept on Palm Island.
(Historical Association of Southern Florida)

145

When Casinos Flourished, and Nobody Cared

He was just a good ol' boy, hardly a candidate for TV stardom. But there, in Miami's federal building under the glare of bright lights, sat Walter Clark, squirming, trying to stay cool, trying to dodge the relentless questions from the Senate Crime Investigating Committee.

The chairman, Estes Kefauver, senator from Tennessee, wanted to parlay the committee's nationally televised hearings into the Democratic nomination for president. He also wanted Walter Clark, ex-butcher, now high sheriff of Broward County, to tell him all about the happy array of 52 illegal gambling casinos operating openly in Broward.

The sheriff, on the other hand, didn't want to tell him anything. After all, he was on the take.

"I don't know" or "I couldn't say" were stock answers, poor lines indeed for America's best daytime television in the summer of 1950.

Asked Chairman Kefauver: "Now, Sheriff Clark, let us get right down to the point of our problem here. In the south end of Broward County, you had operating during the season at various times the Club Greenacres, Colonial Inn, The Club Boheme, and The Farm – and I believe you testified that there were four of five (others) operating in Broward County and have been for quite a number of years, is that right?

Replied Sheriff Clark: "Yes. But not gambling places to my knowledge. They are clubs."

Kefauver: "You have never known that there was gambling in those places?"

Clark: "Rumors, but no actual evidence of it."

The sheriff yielded ground grudgingly; but when the three-day Miami hearings ended, a nationwide TV audience knew that the sheriff of Broward County, Florida, was in cahoots with such charming gangland players as the Lansky brothers, Joe Adonis, Frank Costello, Frank Erickson and Vincent "Jimmy Blue Eyes" Alo.

They also learned that Clark and his brother, Bob, a deputy sheriff, were partners in the Broward Novelty Company, which netted them a sizable income from illegal slot machines and a numbers game called bolita. Bolita alone yielded a quarter-million dollars a year.

The committee's report concluded that Sheriff Clark "completely failed in his duty to enforce the laws of the State of Florida and that he not only aided and abetted violations, but that he personally participated in a major violation."

Thus did America discover that illegal casinos had become as much a part of the South Florida scene as palmetto bugs. Broward, Dade and Palm Beach counties offered something for every kind of wagerer: discreet, exclusive casinos; huge, flashy gambling halls; neighborhood joints; horse-betting parlors; numbers action, even bingo.

These days we have a State Lottery and Florida politicians and voters periodically agonize over whether to

Sheriff Clark in stripes for costume party. *(Fort Lauderdale Historical Society)*

legalize casino gambling; a half-century ago the approach was more direct. Sure, casinos were illegal. But they operated anyway.

Times were tough in the 1930s. Jobs and money were scarce. Gambling casinos separated visiting "swells" from their cash and pumped it back into the sickly local economy. For a few years – from 1935 to 1937 – the state even legalized slot machines; one was installed in the men's room at the Hollywood City Hall.

Casinos meant jobs for the locals – not top jobs as croupiers, but service positions like valet parkers, maintenance men, security guards, barmaids, waiters and cooks. It was estimated that virtually every family in Hallandale,

146

where most of the casinos were concentrated, had at least one paycheck coming in from the gaming industry.

Casino owners and operators and their imported croupiers spent freely, and as a final touch the owners poured generous amounts of money into charitable causes. Casino entertainers were made available for local civic functions. Hallandale's first Policeman's Ball, in the mid-'30s, featured Paul Whiteman, Sophie Tucker, Harry Richman and Joe E. Lewis.

"I was elected on the liberal ticket," said Sheriff Walter Clark, who equated the word "liberal" with "wide-open." In fact, he freely admitted, "I let them have what they want for tourists down here."

People liked Walter Clark because he kept law and order, but never interfered with the fun. He was tough on crimes of violence, tolerant of bootlegging, prostitution and gambling. "Walter Clark knew what was going on, but he regarded these as crimes in name only," recalls Broward author-historian Phil Weidling. "They weren't, he thought, hurting people."

Broward's largest and plushest casinos were in the southern part of the country, just north of the Dade line, so situated to escape the periodic outbursts of righteousness that occasionally punctured Dade's otherwise "liberal" philosophy.

The Colonial Inn was just south of today's Gulfstream Park; Club Boheme at Ocean Drive and Hallandale Beach Boulevard; the Plantation on Hallandale Beach Boulevard, near the Diplomat Mall. Club Greenacres was on Pembroke Road, just west of the Seaboard System Railroad tracks, and The Farm was on Stirling Road at State Road 7, near the bingo halls operated today by the Seminole Tribe.

For a while, Chicago gangster Al Capone leased the Hollywood Country Club as a casino. Fort Lauderdale's best-known gambling den was the It Club, on the south side of town on Southeast 28th Street.

Confiscated Miami slot machines. *(Historical Association of Southern Florida)*

Far from Miami's high-rollers, the casinos in north Broward sought a different kind of clientele. On a spit of land on the Intracoastal Waterway, Capt. Eugene Knight ran the Club Unique in an old fishhouse. His guest list was drawn from the winter visitors at ritzy Hillsboro Club, just across the waterway. Excellent seafood was the big lure at the Club Unique, which even then was called Cap's Place, the name by which it survives today as a Lighthouse Point restaurant.

Three miles up the waterway from Cap's, an old packing house had taken on new life as the River View Club of Deerfield Beach. Run by Bill Stewart, the River View catered to winter guests at the Boca Raton Hotel and Club and the Hillsboro Club. You could make off-track bets on the horses at the Boca Hotel and Club in those days – bookmaking was done in the men's lockerroom and in beach cabanas 147 and 149 – but for casino gambling, the River View was the place.

Stewart was a croupier who had learned his trade at Havana's famed Nacional Hotel. Just like Cap Knight, Stewart served his exclusive clientele first-rate food. Among the 12 to 15 guests each night were members of the Rothschild family and Frederick Rentschler, the founder of Pratt & Whitney Aircraft, who always called ahead to order stone crabs.

The action was a good deal rougher in south Broward. In Hallandale, a huge packing shed surrounded by fields of cabbages and tomatoes was turned into the Old Plantation, a barnlike structure, undecorated and unpainted. The Plantation was operated by "Potatoes" Kaufman, representing the Chicago mob. Roulette, chuck-a-luck, blackjack and craps drew wagerers from all over the area. Bingo games were held at night.

Somewhere along the way Potatoes offended people in power. He simply disappeared. He was generally believed to have been dropped into the Gulf Stream wearing cement overshoes.

The Colonial Inn, also in Hallandale, was as fancy as Plantation was plain, decorated ostentatiously in burgundy, red, gold and white with deep-pile carpeting and red velvet draperies. Action was heavy; half a million dollars might cross the tables in one night. Comic Joe E. Lewis was master of ceremonies at the Colonial's stage shows, which featured such headliners as Carmen Miranda, Jane Froman and Ray Bolger, the kindly Scarecrow from the Land of Oz. Built by gambler Frank Costello, the Colonial soon became the property of mobsters Meyer and Jake Lansky.

Big Jack Letendre set up La Boheme in competition with the Colonial. "Persons unknown" tried to buy him out. He refused. Big Jack was shot dead in his home in Woonsocket, Rhode Island. Jake Lansky wound up running La Boheme.

In Dade County, Miami's casinos presented elaborate stage extravaganzas. The Latin Quarter featured the flashy and fleshy creations of showman Lou Walters, whose daughter, Barbara, would prove to be even better on television than either Senator Kefauver or Sheriff Clark.

The Royal Palm Club's payoff to authorities was reported to be as high as $25,000 a week, not unreasonable for an operation grossing up to $2 million a night. The war ended the club's glory days in 1941. It was requisitioned as a barracks for Coast Guardsmen. After the war, it burned down.

In general, cash payoffs for protection against raids or harassment were good for no more than seven days. The name of one large Miami gambling syndicate reflects the uncertainty of such short-term arrangements. It was called the S & G Syndicate – S & G for "stop and go."

While Dade and Broward casinos operated across a broad range of styles, from sleazy to ritzy, sedate Palm Beach met the phenomenon of illegal gambling with a casino so proper no one would even dream of calling it illegal. At least not often.

For 48 years, Col. E.R. Bradley's Beach Club operated in Palm Beach – the longest known run of any illegal casino in this country. From 1898 to 1946, he was raided just once – and the lawman who blundered was quickly persuaded to pursue the case no further.

Clad in a dark suit, dark tie, white shirt and high, stiff choke-collar, Bradley ran a casino where correct, conservative behavior was demanded. Members dressed in formal wear. Noisy outbursts were met with arched eyebrows. Heavy drinking was discouraged, as was smoking.

Bradley's elegant clientele included the rich and famous of America, a clientele so wealthy that his betting limits were higher than the less-exclusive but more famous Monte Carlo. As much as $50,000 might ride on the turn of a card.

Membership was limited to non-Florida residents, to eliminate the charge that the casino was taking money out of local pockets. Members had to be at least 25, and they had to be blessed with the capacity to lose enormous sums of money without noisy protests. If a member even hinted that he had been cheated, his losses were refunded immediately. At the same time his membership card was torn in two. He was no longer privileged to lose his silk shirt at Bradley's – which was a blackballing of serious magnitude in the social world of Palm Beach.

Bradley's has been described as "a chaste, white, wooden house." Its color scheme inside and out was white and green, also the colors of his racing silks at his Idle Hour Farm, America's most successful racing stable at the time. His was the first stable to saddle four Kentucky Derby winners.

A realist, the Colonel protected his casino not only from any rash moves by the law but also from the threats of those outside the law. An armed 30-man security force, carefully trained, covered the casino inside and out, bolstered by a solitary rifleman concealed behind lattice work above the "ballroom," as the gambling area was called. Bradley kept a half a million dollars in his safe; his guests may have carried more than that into the casino. The temptation must have been great, but no gunmen ever dared to test Bradley's elaborate defenses.

Bradley protected himself from attack in other ways,

148

Colonel Bradley's Beach Club, 1925. *(Historical Society of Palm Beach County)*

too. At one time he controlled the *Palm Beach Post* and the *Palm Beach Times*, the county's only daily newspapers. And to guard against criticism from the pulpit, he gave generously to area churches, particularly St. Edwards's Catholic Church, which was named after him. A devout Catholic, he closed his casino on Sunday and led his croupiers and restaurant staff in a group to attend Mass.

His generosity to local churches did not shield him, however, from the stings of the famous touring evangelist, Bob Jones.

"If I were an officer of the law, I'd close that place or die," Jones declared. "I hope if I were to come back here after 25 years I'd find there had been officers with enough stamina and grit to do their duty. They go and arrest a poor man for playing poker and let those millionaires gamble unmolested."

When the colonel died in 1946, he willed that the club be torn down and replaced with a town park. The timing of his death was fitting. The era of Florida's illegal casinos was coming to an end.

Crusading editors at the *Fort Lauderdale News* and *The Miami Herald* began exposing gambling. The City of Fort Lauderdale started arresting and fining bookmakers. On Feb. 12, 1948 Dwight Rogers Jr., assistant state attorney, went to circuit court and brought a civil injunction against the Colonial, Greenacres and the Lopez Restaurant.

In Hollywood, Lee Wentworth, former tax assessor, led a citizens' group in a crusade against gambling. Jake Lansky called on him and offered a $25,000 bribe. Wentworth ignored it.

A few nights later, three Lansky aides showed up with a shoebox. One said: "We have $25,000 here. You know how these things end – either with a silver bullet or a silver dollar."

Wentworth went back into his house. When he came out, he carried a shotgun. "I'm going to count to five and then I'm going to start shooting," he said. Lansky's men drove off, and never returned.

The Kefauver road show of 1950 brought more pressure. After the hearings, Gov. Fuller Warren suspended Sheriff Clark and the Broward County grand jury brought 14 indictments against the lawman.

Suffering from leukemia, Clark was a dying man when he came to trial. He was acquitted on all counts – predictable, perhaps, because he represented the will of the people. Within a year he was dead, and Broward's wide-open days died with him.

149

PART SEVEN

Pipe Dreams and Nightmares

City for Sale, Ten Dollars an Acre

Arthur Williams was a boy of 13, traveling with his surveyor father, when he first saw the New River. It was 1870, and the river wound through a lushly tropical land that was virtually deserted.

Seventeen years later, Williams came back from Jacksonville to start Broward County's first development. He called it Palm City.

Williams bought 100 acres from the Florida Land and Mortgage Company, a British firm with vast holdings in South Florida. Williams' parcels extended about two miles along the south side of the New River, west of today's Federal Highway.

When he platted Palm City in 1887, Williams knew he would have to rely heavily on out-of-town sales. the whole area had only one white settler, and he already had a house to live in – the sailors' House of Refuge where he was the keeper.

Williams kicked off his sales campaign with an ad in the *Jacksonville Times-Union* which read:

"We are now selling lots in Palm City for ten dollars each, 50 x 100, and pay cost of recording and taxes for two years. If you are looking for an opportunity to secure a good home where a good living can be reasonably earned, where land is high and choice, where climate is invigorating and delightful, and a point where land is valuable and sure to rapidly enhance in value, we suggest to you with confidence an investment in Palm City lots."

From the ad, Williams sold 26 lots. Because his sales pitch had agreed to pay the taxes for the first two years, it was not until the third year that buyers began forfeiting their land for nonpayment of taxes. In 1890 five blocks of land were sold for $1.20 at a tax sale.

By 1894, Williams' company was selling land, when it could, as acreage, ignoring the plat that he had hoped would serve as the blueprint for a city on the shores of the New River. Despite his dreams, Williams never got rich from the land.

Not until the boom of the 1920s was his site selection deemed visionary. Then, the land that had been Palm City became Croissant Park, Fort Lauderdale's biggest boomtime development.

Arthur Williams. *(Fort Lauderdale Historical Society)*

Cyrus Teed and the Koreshans

Transpose two numbers and 1984, the year of George Orwell's novel becomes 1894, the year that Cyrus Read Teed, as Big Brotherly a presence as Florida has ever known, set up shop here.

In 1894, Dr. Teed, a Chicago physician, founded New Jerusalem, a Koreshan Unity commune on the Estero River, just south of Fort Myers. He platted a new city with streets 400 feet wide, and dreamed one day of accommodating eight million Koreshans on the southwest coast of Florida.

Teed's followers totalled 4,000, and of that number only 200 moved to Florida as converts of one of the most bizarre philosophies of the 19th century, a time when strange Utopian communities were springing up around the country.

To Teed and the Koreshans, the universe was one giant cell, a hollow sphere with a circumference of 25,000 miles. Earthlings did not live on the exterior surface, gazing

Cyrus Read Teed. *(Seeman Publishing)*

upward at heavens stretching into infinity. Instead, Teed believed that our dwelling place was on the *inside* of the cell. The sun, moon and stars were apparently all in there with us.

In his book, *Cellular Cosmogony,* Teed contended that the interior surface of the earth was concave, with a curvature of eight inches to the mile. In 1896, he organized a geodetic expedition to put his theory to the test. His survey, conducted just south of the Naples pier, convinced his followers, who already believed. Outsiders were unimpressed.

Cyrus in Hebrew is *Koresh,* hence the name Koreshan to describe the movement launched by Teed, whom the Chicago *Herald* called "an undersized, smooth-shaven man whose brown, restless eyes glow and burn like live coals."

Besides the universal cell doctrine, the Koreshans did not believe in a competitive, capitalistic society. Thus, all converts were required to sign over all their earthly belongings to Koreshan Unity.

Men and women alike had to give up alcohol and tobacco and, probably hardest of all, they had to give up each other. Koreshans lived celibate lives, the men and women in separate dormitories. How they planned to continue their community into a second generation was never explained.

Koreshans spent much of their time baking bread, pursuing agriculture with great skill and even publishing an excellent paper, *The American Eagle,* which became an important Florida horticultural publication. They were active politically in the affairs of Lee County, but they were not fanatics. Technically speaking, they were communists, but they could hardly be described as Marxists. Within their own community and in their dealings with the outside world, Koreshans were gentle, kindly folk.

In December 1908, Dr. Teed presented his followers with a real dilemma. Although he had claimed to be immortal, he died, at age 69.

Convinced he would rise again, his followers kept watch over Teed's body. The county health agent told them they would have to bury him. So Teed's body was placed in a bathtub and sealed in a brick and concrete tomb at the east end of Estero Island. In 1921, a hurricane washed his tomb away.

After his death the movement, deprived of Teed's charismatic leadership, slowly decayed. Today, the old site of New Jerusalem is Koreshan State Park, a peaceful, beautifully landscaped reminder of a time when the followers of Cyrus Teed lived a life of celibacy on the inside of the earth's crust.

Visitors at Koreshan State Park. *(John Curry, Sunshine Magazine)*

Alexander Took Fort Lauderdale to the Beach

Drive east of Las Olas Boulevard and you'll find some of Fort Lauderdale's finest shops, boutiques and restaurants. It's a superbly-landscaped street with an artsy personality all its own. Many consider it Fort Lauderdale at its best.

Today, the boulevard extends without interruption from downtown Fort Lauderdale to the ocean. Getting the road across to the beach was not an easy task. Early settlers to the area didn't find the ocean all that inviting.

At the turn of the century, the land known now as the Bartlett Estate and Hugh Taylor Birch State Park was owned by Birch, a wealthy Chicago lawyer and part-time recluse. Between the Birch property and the Fort Lauderdale House of Refuge on the south end of the beach lay 32 acres owned by Tom Watson, a Georgia publisher and 1904 Populist Party candidate for president.

Everybody else lived on the mainland, mostly along the New River. The land was better for farming, the river provided safe harbor for a boat and your house was less likely to be blown away by a hurricane.

D.C. Alexander did not share the prevailing coolness toward oceanfront property. He had lived in California where he observed the joys of beachside living.

For $40,000, Alexander bought Watson's 32 acres and his hunting lodge, built in the shape of a gun. He converted the lodge into the Las Olas Inn, the beach's first hotel, and built a bathing pavillion.

The problem in 1914 was how to get to the beach. Since boats were the only practical answer, Alexander found a shortage of people rushing over to buy lots at Las Olas By-The-Sea.

A stock company was formed to build a bridge over the Intracoastal Waterway and to finish Las Olas Boulevard, but its efforts failed. In 1915, Broward County faced up to the problem, voting its first bond issue, for $400,000, to build bridges across the Intracoastal at Fort Lauderdale, Deerfield, Pompano, Dania and Hallandale and an overland road and bridges to Davie.

In January 1917, the road to the beach was opened to the public. Virtually every vehicle in Fort Lauderdale was recruited for a giant motorcade.

Alexander's lots were now salable – he sold 20 the year the bridge opened.

Opening up his oceanfront development, Alexander made one enormous contribution to the future of his adopted town. In platting Las Olas, he established an oceanside street, Atlantic Boulevard, well back from the water. He permitted no structures east of the road.

His concept preserved for the public the single natural feature which would in time become the town's most important attraction – Fort Lauderdale Beach.

Las Olas Boulevard, ca. 1915. *(Fort Lauderdale Historical Society)*

Tamiami Trail Blazers

These days, crossing the Everglades isn't all that difficult. You can hop in the car and drive across Alligator Alley or, farther to the south, the Tamiami Trail. It was not always thus.

In 1915, J.F. Jaudon, Dade County tax assessor and real estate developer, was promoting a highway from Miami to Fort Myers and then on up to Tampa. A man from Tampa suggested it be called the Tamiami Trail.

From opposite sides of South Florida, Dade and Lee County authorities set about building the Trail in their areas, hoping to connect at some future date. Eight years later that date was still way off and the project was badly bogged down, with a 40-mile gap of Everglades and cypress swamp separating the completed parts.

A group of Fort Myers civic and business leaders decided that a dramatic gesture was needed to revive interest in the Trail. They dubbed themselves the Trail Blazers, and their goal was somehow to make it across the gap via automobile, thereby proving that crossing the Everglades by car was possible.

On April 4, 1923, the Trail Blazers, 25 in all, including two Indian guides, set out from Fort Myers. The caravan consisted of eight Fords, a commissary truck and a 3,200-pound Elcar, entered in the event by a car dealer to prove the vehicle's stamina. The Elcar did fine on the parts of the Trail already completed but it lasted only about 100 yards into the really rough going. It had to be tugged the rest of the way by two tractors.

The trip, planned to take three days, took three weeks. Planes went out to search for the Blazers and failed to spot them. Wild stories circulated. The group was lost in quicksand. They had been captured and tortured by Indians. One story claimed they had taken several women with them and were simply in no hurry to get out.

The truth was a good deal less glamorous. The cars kept sinking into the muck, wheels were broken, an engine burned out. The men had to build makeshift bridges and cut down saplings to lay out a "corduroy" road of wood.

Finally, mosquito-bitten, sawgrass-slashed, famished and weary, the Trail Blazers reached Dade County.

Did their trail blazing speed up completion of the first road across the Everglades? Possibly. At any rate, the Tamiami Trail was finally opened to the public in April, 1928 – just five years after the Trail Blazers ended their adventure.

Building the Tamiami Trail, ca. 1925. *(Historical Association of Southern Florida)*

155

Joe Young's Hollywood: Traffic Circles, the Broadwalk and Tent City

Before developer Joseph W. Young arrived on the scene in 1920, the open space between Dania and Hallandale was nothing more than farmland, wetlands and, east of the Intracoastal Waterway, sandy beach.

Young, a 300-pounder biographers describe as a super-salesman, purchased all the coastal land, and from the start developed his new city of Hollywood through a master plan, not just a scattershot grouping of unrelated subdivisions. Addressing salesmen in his native Indianapolis, he began platting the city from rough sketches drawn on the backs of envelopes.

"Here," he told them, "will be a wide boulevard extending from the ocean westward to the edge of the Everglades. Here, one on each side of the boulevard and opening into the Intracoastal canal, we'll create two lakes, each with a turning basin for yachts..."

Young, who later formed the Hollywood Land and Water Company to develop the tract, also planned the central business section, sites for school, churches, golf courses and parks.

"This will be a city for everyone – from the opulent at the top of the industrial and society ladders to the most humble of working people," he said.

Hollywood Boulevard was designed by Young's organization to be "Florida's widest paved street." It was 120 feet wide, including sidewalks, graded and filled with a bed of ojus (Dade County limestone rock). The boulevard was not topped with asphalt but in 1924 was oiled and lit with clusters of round streetlights.

Today, motorists bound for other places curse the three

Joseph W. Young. *(Fort Lauderdale Historical Society)*

Hollywood Boulevard, 1925. *(Fort Lauderdale Historical Society)*

circles on Hollywood Boulevard that confuse and slow them down as they drive through Broward County's second largest city.

Young would have nodded approval. That's why he built the circles – to keep the showcase boulevard in his "Dream City" from becoming a speedway. And give Young credit for knowing the potential of the motorcar to change cities for the worse.

Young had other reasons, too. He liked the symmetry that the circles gave to his grand plan for Hollywood. Additionally, he wanted centrally-located space for parks and public buildings. Young was also influenced by the downtown circles he grew up with in Indianapolis. He had developed property there and in Arizona and California, but nothing on the scale of Hollywood, Florida, which was his first and only planned community.

The circle where J.W. Young Memorial Park sits today was originally named Harding Circle for Warren G. Harding, president at the time it was begun. In 1948, the Hollywood City Commission adopted a resolution to change the name to honor their city's founder.

Today, just as J.W. envisioned, Hollywood Boulevard stretches from the ocean to the Everglades. Young would probably not be pleased, however, to learn that along its route the boulevard briefly relinquishes its name to Pines Boulevard in Pembroke Pines, before becoming Hollywood again as it continues west to U.S. 27.

And he was certainly not pleased when the bust hit in 1926, and, like other developers all over Florida, he lost his city to the paving contractor whom he had selected to build the "wide road" of his dreams.

Atlantic City made the boardwalk famous when it built its seven-mile walkway along the Jersey shore more than a century ago.

Joe Young wanted beachside strollers at his "Dream City" to enjoy a similar walkway. Only instead of wood he used concrete, confident it would prove more durable. But, what to call it? Boardwalk certainly didn't apply, since no boards were used. The solution was to call it "Broadwalk."

"I don't know who actually came up with the name," says L.B. "Slats" Slater, a Hollywood Realtor who was a friend of Young's in the heady days of the great Florida land boom. "It may have been Young himself. It shows up as "Broadwalk" even on the earlier drawings."

Young's construction crews were busy, too, building the Hollywood Hotel, the Tangerine Tea Room, a new sales pavillion and a huge bathhouse, swimming pool, casino complex, all of them fronting on the two-mile-long Broadwalk. It became the place to go – to swim, to stroll or to see and be seen.

In July, 1926 the first hurricane to hit southeast Florida since 1910 came ashore. The ocean roared across the Broadwalk. J.W. Young's indestructible concrete proved decidedly destructible. Part of the old original Broadwalk lies at the bottom of the Intracoastal Waterway.

Fortunately, the City of Hollywood rebuilt it and today the two-mile stretch is solidly established as the Hollywood institution Young wanted it to be.

Hollywood Beach Broadwalk, 1925. *(Hollywood Historical Society)*

Young's Hollywood grew so rapidly that by the mid-1920s, his people were claiming it had become Broward's biggest city.

To meet the demand for hotel space, Young came up with a novel idea: "Tent City," a row of tents near the ocean that would provide temporary lodging for winter visitors. The rare photograph published here gives only a hint of Tent City's charm.

Staying in Tent City was a far cry from camping in the woods. These were luxury accommodations, with beautifully furnished living rooms, bedrooms, bathrooms and kitchenettes.

Several hundred tents were erected in orderly rows, with

Tent City on Hollywood Beach. *(Fort Lauderdale Historical Society)*

street lights every 50 feet or so. Naturally, J.W. provided maid service.

But the tourists who filled the tents in the 1925-26 winter season, and who reveled in the joys of the Roaring Twenties, barely missed an event which could have put a definite damper on their vacations.

The same 1926 hurricane that destroyed the Broadwalk blew Tent City to smithereens.

It was never rebuilt.

Galt Had His Mile and Blacks Had a Beach

Today the Galt Ocean Mile is lined with high-rise condominiums, a remarkable concentration of luxury dwellings valued at hundreds of millions of dollars. But a half century ago it was far from a prime property. The politicians that ran the city considered it so expendable that it was the only beach area that Fort Lauderdale's black population was allowed to use.

The story and the name of Ocean Mile began in 1913, when Arthur Galt, a Chicago lawyer, bought the property. It took him 40 years to sell it, not that he needed to; Galt was the son of the law partner of Hugh Taylor Birch, who at one time owned most of what is today's Fort Lauderdale Beach.

Incredibly, the Ocean Mile was only part of the land that Galt purchased, although most of the 8,000 acres that was included lay west of the Intracoastal Waterway. It was during the 1920's, the glorious days of Florida's land boom, that the countess of Lauderdale, Gwendolyn Maitland, decided to create a resort to rival Palm Beach, except she was going to do it in Fort Lauderdale.

To that end, the slim, refined-looking Scot formed the British Improvement Association, which promptly began acquiring property, principally a successful subdivision called Oakland Park and 8,000 acres from Galt. The down payment for Galt's property was one million dollars, while the total price the countess and her group laid out was seven million.

She had assembled an impressive group of partners: two lords, a viscount, an ex-king of Greece and a number of her fellow aristocratic Palm Beachers, including society's ruling grande dame, Mrs. E.T. Stotesbury.

The new resort town, incorporated on November 25, 1925, was called Floranada, a combination of Florida and Canada. The cornerstone was laid for the Floranada Inn, a golf course was built and a narrow-gauge railway was ordered.

Then came the bust, the inglorious end to Florida's great land boom. The company had sold only a few lots and the money on these was refunded and the land reverted to Galt.

At this point, no one was interested in buying, but when, in 1927, the last remaining oceanfront public beaches in the city of Fort Lauderdale were declared off limits to blacks, by default they used the Ocean Mile, which became known as the "black beach."

Galt was choosy about selling his land. Prospective buyers had to promise building programs that met his standards. He once turned down an otherwise good offer when he found the land would be used for a trailer park.

After World War II, James S. Hunt and Stephen Calder formed a partnership and persuaded Galt to sell them a parcel of land between Middle River and the Intracoastal. They called it Coral Ridge and dubbed their company Coral Ridge Properties.

In time, Galt sold them the last 2,400 acres, including the Galt Ocean Mile. The price was $19,389,000, at that time the largest private land transaction in the history of the United States.

For blacks, it meant moving on to another beach, south of the Port Everglades Inlet. For the Ocean Mile that Galt had held for four decades, it meant the beginning of its decidedly new, high-rise look.

Galt Ocean Mile as it looked in 1942. *(Coral Ridge Properties)*

An Opa-locka Fantasy

Some say it was the vision of Glenn Curtiss that brought Baghdad to Miami. Others suspect nightmare might have been a better way to describe the wild dreams that excited the famed aviation pioneer in 1925. Blame it on the Florida land boom.

How else do you explain a man who built a town of minarets and domes intersected with streets named Aladdin, Sesame, Caliph, Ali Baba, Sinbad and Sharazad (short for *Scheherazade*)?

Curtiss was a great one for shortening things. The Seminoles called the land where he built his town Opatishawockalocka. Glenn named it Opa-locka.

Curtiss also shortened the time it took to get from one place to another. The motorcycles he built were the fastest and he set world speed records in his airplanes.

During World War I, Curtiss made more than 30 million dollars building planes. This left him with a strong capital position when the mania of the Florida land boom engulfed him. At the time he was operating an airfield and a ranch near Miami.

Curtiss and ranching partner James Bright subdivided part of the ranch and sold it. It became Hialeah. Next they brought Pueblo Indian architecture to Florida in a town now called Miami Springs.

By this time, Curtiss, his 18 corporations and the boom were flying high. For Opa-locka, he engaged a famous New York architect to forge new frontiers in the architec-ture of fantasy. Bernhard E. Muller came up with a Robin Hood-style English village anchored with a medieval castle. But that was not to be.

"Oh, Glenn, it's just like a scene from the Arabian Nights," said a Curtiss relative. Curtiss promptly sent Muller a copy of *The Thousand and One Nights* to use as his guide.

What followed was an incredible journey into the world of the imagination. From a land where Seminoles had roamed rose a town from another world and time. The Opa-locka Company's administration building, a mosque-like structure with domes, minarets and arches, was inspired by a description of the palace of Emperor Kosroushah in the tale of *The Talking Bird*.

The Seaboard train station was crowned with twin domes and decorated with elaborately-tiled archways. Homes and apartments, public buildings, a bank, a hotel – all bore the stamp of the Arabian Nights. More than 90 buildings had been completed by 1930, the year Curtiss died.

Today, the company's administration building is the Opa-locka City Hall, from which the city fathers are embarking on a plan to restore and preserve Curtiss' weird "Dream of Araby."

Opa-locka Administration Building, late 1920s. *(Historical Association of Southern Florida)*

The Great Oil Boom That Wasn't

It started prophetically enough. Swimmers in the New River noticed bubbles which burst and spread out, creating an oil slick. Could it be oil beneath Fort Lauderdale?

In 1927, a group of businessmen trapped a sample of the gas in a bottle. Back in realtor M.A. Hortt's office they found that it burned with what Hortt called "a beautiful blue flame."

An analysis of the gas by the Pittsburgh Testing Laboratory confirmed that it was in fact natural gas, and almost immediately Fort Lauderdale went on its first and only bout of "oil fever" – a fever so intense that a picture of an oil rig appeared on the city's 1929 tax bills.

Speculators rushed to secure oil leases. Two geologists were hired to conduct surveys. Oil, they said, would probably be found on both sides of the New River at a depth of 6,500 feet.

The Port Everglades Gas & Oil Co. was organized and began drilling in Croissant Park south of the river at SW 4th Avenue and 14th Court.

Investors scraped together enough money to buy a large oil rig. Hundreds turned out to watch the commencement of drilling on Jan. 21, 1929. When the drilling reached 1,000 feet the money ran out. A second canvass for funds pushed the drill down to 2,000 feet. A gas pocket along the way lifted the spirits of the citizenry for still another thousand feet. And that's where the money and the drilling stopped – at 3,101 feet.

The rig was removed and the well abandoned. All that remained was the expensive metal casing left behind in the dry hole.

During World War II, when metal was in short supply, a Cuban oilman learned of the abandoned casing and set off a charge of nitroglycerine to remove it. A geyser of water erupted, which the Frank Medford family, who owned land adjacent to the well, began using to irrigate their plants.

The gusher turned out to be rich in minerals. Now it was the town's turn to get excited about mineral water. In 1950, the Fort Lauderdale Spa Co. was formed. It lasted three years. Later, the mineral waters surfaced again as the Cloud Nine Spa, described as one of the city's "in places" in 1967.

And today? Appropriately, the site is now headquarters for the Broward County Environmental Quality Control Board.

Drilling for oil in Croissant Park, south of the New River, 1929. *(Fort Lauderdale Historical Society)*

Boca's Ten Days of the Camel

Boca Raton's leaders would probably cast a suspicious eye on anyone who told them they could attract more attention to their city if they built a giant camel across its major thoroughfare. Attracting attention is not a problem for booming Boca. But it was not always so. And once there *was* a giant camel, and later a sort of elk, sitting astride Dixie Highway.

On April 4, 1928, a stalwart pillar of the Boca Raton establishment, J.C. Mitchell, appeared before the town council with a mad scheme. Representing the chamber of commerce, Mitchell asked the council to appropriate $1,000 to build a wooden camel to stand astride Dixie. No one driving south or north, Mitchell reasoned, could miss it.

Did the council laugh at Mitchell? No way. Within a week they had approved his bizarre proposal unanimously and moved briskly ahead to get additional approvals from the Palm Beach County Commission and the Florida East Coast Railway, on whose right-of-way the camel would perch.

Why would the commissioners opt for the camel? The answer is simple: They were desperately seeking publicity for a town that in 1928 was unknown outside of South Florida.

In the spring of 1928, the Shriners were scheduled to hold their national convention in Miami. Since the only north-south highway was Dixie, Shriners who drove down to Miami would have to motor through the camel, one of the symbols of their huge lodge. And, the thinking went, how could they ever forget the little town at the southern end of Palm Beach County?

So, the huge camel was built from two-by-fours covered with beaver-board and painted. It was supported by cables, guy wires and braces. Cramer & Cramer, builders of the town hall, erected this unlikely ship of the desert.

H.M. Rodabaugh, the FEC Railway vice president who gave his consent, must have been intrigued by the project. On April 30, 1928, he sent this telegram to the Boca Raton mayor: "I saw your camel as I passed through Boca Raton this evening stop It makes a fine appearance stop I congratulate you on your enterprise (sic)."

All the "stops" in Rodabaugh's telegram weren't enough to stop the madness. Not to be outdone by the Shriners, the Elks Club got into the act, approving a total of $540 to transform the camel into an elk, presumably to startle passing Elks. It might have evolved to other animal forms, except that the city permit only lasted ten days.

After that, the camel and the elk were history.

Boca Raton's camel. *(Boca Raton Historical Society)*

Going Batty on Sugarloaf Key

All anyone remembers about Richter Clyde Perky is a little settlement in the Florida Keys called Perky – and a bat tower.

It's an unusual legacy for a man whose dream of a boomtime resort was swept away in cloud after cloud of fierce salt-march mosquitos.

A Coloradan, Perky bought nearly all of Sugarloaf Key in 1919 for $10,000 and brought his considerable land development and sales skills to bear on the island venture. But he didn't count on blood-thirsty mosquitos attacking visitors, making Sugarloaf Key virtually uninhabitable.

Perky reacted with a bold move. He had heard of the work of Dr. Charles Campbell, a San Antonio physician, who had sought to hold down the population of malarial mosquitos by bringing bats in to eat them. His ideas were presented in many scholarly journals and in a 1925 book, *Bats, Mosquitos and Dollars.*

Dr. Campbell had designed and patented a special bat tower to serve as a home for friendly, mosquito-munching bats. Perky should have been more wary. One of the good doctor's seven towers was erected on the grounds of an insane asylum, perhaps a check on the bats-in-the-belfry syndrome.

In between swats, Perky bought plans and bat bait from the Texan. He built two 30-foot, cedar-shingled towers of Dade County pine. Above the flat Lower Keys landscape the towers loomed like windmills without blades.

Campbell also sold Perky a magical potion of bat bait, a loathsome concoction of bat droppings and ground-up sex organs of female bats. It was shipped in a small pine box like a coffin.

Placed on the earthen floors of the towers, the bat bait was allowed to go to work. Nose-witness accounts describe the smell as so sickening that people working nearby had to keep their distance. So did the bats.

There is no evidence that any bat ever roomed at the towers. And yet, the towers and the bat bait cost Perky more than he paid for the island itself.

Legend has it that Keys mosquitos ate the bats, not the other way around. At any rate, the mosquito problem was never solved until massive spraying of the Keys years later.

Today one of Perky's towers still stands, designated a historic landmark. An inscription on its base reads: "Dedicated to good health at Perky, Fla., by Mr. and Mrs. R.C. Perky, March 15, 1929."

The Bat Tower. *(Florida Photographic Archives)*

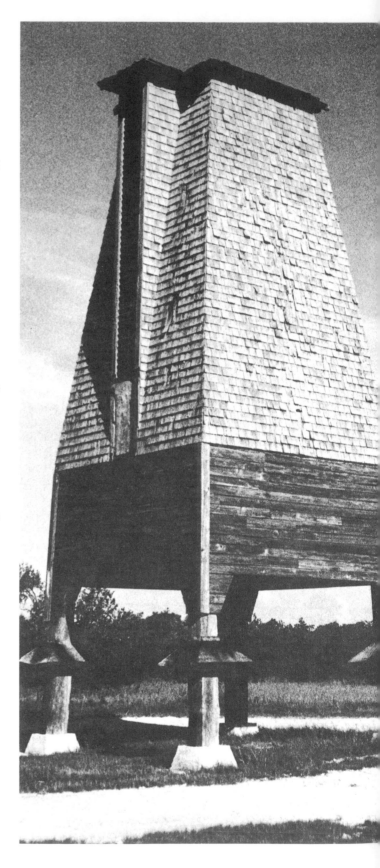

Selling Shares of the Grove

There's always been something distinctive about Flamingo Groves, in West Broward on Flamingo Road. It dates all the way back to the days when the groves were planted in 1927.

Floyd Wray had been a member of the high-powered sales force recruited by Joseph B. Young to sell houses and lots in Hollywood-by-the-Sea during the heady days of the great Florida land boom. Young's salesmen were good at their jobs, but the jobs vanished overnight after the bust and the hurricane of 1926.

Wray and his wife Jane managed to scrape together a little money, then teamed up with horticulturist Frank Stirling to buy 320 acres of prime hammock land in Davie from Frank Mittie Chaplin. Wray pulled together a strong nine-man sales team, hiring such Hollywood-by-the-Sea luminaries as C.P. Hammerstein.

Their job was to sell groveland, using an approach never before seen in South Florida. Adapting a citrus condominium program already operating at Howie-in-the-Hills in Central Florida, the Flamingo folks platted their property into five-acre units which were sold on five-year contracts for $750 each.

The corporation then planted the five-acre parcels in citrus trees and contracted to spray, fertilize and prune them. After five years the condo owners had the option of selling the units back to Flamingo at a specified price or of receiving a pro-rated share of the profits from the overall crop.

Making sure the trees thrived was the responsibility of Stirling, with advice from famed horticulturist David Fairchild, founder of Miami's Fairchild Tropical Garden.

Stirling, Davie's first mayor, brought strong credentials to the job himself. He had come to Davie as a member of the U.S. Department of Agriculture and the Florida State Plant Board to help stamp out the citrus canker blight in the mid-1920s. Stirling planted some 70 varieties of citrus trees at Flamingo Groves.

Soon after the commercial operation started, the Flamingo Groves Botanical Garden was established. By 1931 the first fruit shipping center was opened on Hollywood Boulevard. The first packing plant was built in 1934, and later moved to Federal Highway near the railroad into Port Everglades.

Even during the Depression, Floyd Wray's share-cropping condo groves moved ahead. The future had never looked brighter for the Broward citrus industry. Wray could not have foreseen that someday condominiums for people would take over groveland he might have sold as condos for oranges.

Orange harvest at Flamingo Groves in Davie, ca. 1950. *(Fort Lauderdale Historical Society)*

Clyde Beatty's Fort Lauderdale Zoo

Today Fort Lauderdale's Gateway Shopping Center stands at a location on East Sunrise Boulevard where lions once roamed and roared in the night.

Back in the 1930's, Clyde Beatty was one of America's most famous wild animal trainers. He toured the country as a circus performer and starred in such Hollywood extravaganzas as *The Big Cage* and *The Lost Jungle*.

On vacation in Fort Lauderdale in November of 1938, Beatty and his wife Harriet were driving along Federal Highway, north of the Fort Lauderdale city limits. Suddenly he saw a sign that read "Lion Farm."

A sign like that was bound to catch the eye of a man who made his living taming big cats. What Beatty found was the McKillop-Hutton Lion Farm, established in 1935 on the site of a former rock pit. As lion farms go, it was not flourishing; in fact, the farm was down to its last five lions.

The following spring Beatty bought the lion farm plus some adjacent land. He invested $85,000 in grottos, miniature mountains, lush tropical vegetation and a four-story waterfall.

On December 2, 1939, the Clyde Beatty Jungle Zoo opened its gates. As Fort Lauderdale's first major tourist attraction, it featured lagoons, a waterfall and a plentiful complement of the great mammals of Africa and Asia. Circus acts were performed each afternoon and evening at the 25-acre complex.

For five years the Beattys lived happily in a growing Fort Lauderdale. But that was the problem. Fort Lauderdale was growing so fast that the Beatty Zoo found itself surrounded by houses and apartments. It also found itself *inside* the city limits of Fort Lauderdale. New residents, many of whom had no circus in their blood, began complaining. The lions roared at night and monkeys roamed through the trees in the neighborhood.

Beatty and the zoo were there first, but homeowners have more votes than tigers. The city commission caved in and passed a law prohibiting wild animals inside the city limits.

The new law destroyed the Clyde Beatty Jungle Zoo. Three years later, the property was condemned and all structures, cages and fences were torn down. The land was sold to a group of businessmen who built the Gateway Shopping Center.

Beatty returned to Broward County briefly in the winter of 1960-61 to operate an attraction called Clyde Beatty's Jungleland on U.S.1, south of Hollywood. It was too late. The days were gone when a wild animal attraction could thrive in densely-populated East Broward.

Entrance to Clyde Beatty's Zoo. *(Fort Lauderdale Historical Society)*

Once Upon a Time in Pompano

Three decades ago, Storyland was the roadside attraction home of a dazzling assortment of childhood celebrities: Little Bo Peep, Jack and Jill, Little Boy Blue and Rip Van Winkle. It was, long before Disney came to Florida, a land of multi-colored plaster buildings designed to fulfill kids' fantasies as it emptied their parents' wallets.

Storyland was conceived by Sydney C. Caswell, a retired General Electric executive, and Al Hennessy, an advertising man from Dania. Painstaking research through illustrations for countless fairy tales preceded the design of the buildings.

The attraction was built on a ten-acre island in Pompano Beach, surrounded by a type of waterway that Floridians have come to call a canal. In Storyland parlance it was a "moat." Visitors crossed a wooden "drawbridge" to what looked from the road like a castle with minarets.

Storyland opened on November 25, 1955. Children loved it. Parents were less enthusiastic about the fee structure. One fee was paid going in, another coming out. The second fee was based on how many individual rides and multi-colored plaster houses kids could shame their parents into visiting. The exit fee was hard to control and it could sometimes mount up steeply.

In less than a decade Storyland had lost its appeal. Bob Mayes, of Mayes Chevrolet, bought the property in 1964 to expand his automobile dealership. A few months later, Hurricane Cleo came barreling through and smashed the dreamscape beyond repair.

Some of the debris was used for fill as Mayes closed in the southern and eastern parts of the moat. Clint Fowlkes, son of C.J. Fowlkes, secretary-treasurer of Mayes Chevrolet, recalls those days:

Storyland. *(Broward County Historical Commission)*

"I can remember parking extra cars back in Storyland. I remember the house of the Old Woman in a Shoe. It became a hangout for winos. In time everything had to be torn down."

Now the land west of Federal Highway and just south of Cypress Creek in Pompano Beach is home for a car dealer, and along the water, the Waterford Point condo.

Nothing remains of Storyland except a few pictures and a lot of memories. Among those who remember is Pompano Beach clothier E. Grey Webb, who summed Storyland up this way:

"It was fun, I guess – sort of a rinky-dink Disney World."

Storyland from the air, ca. 1955. *(Fran Zent, C.J. Fowlkes)*

Africa USA in Boca Raton

Today it's home for affluent Boca Ratonians who enjoy living in the lushly landscaped acres of Camino Gardens.

Once it was home for an assortment of African animals. Zebras roamed through the area, as did giraffes, elephants, cheetahs and monkeys. This was Africa USA, one of South Florida's best-known tourist attractions.

In 1960 *Life* magazine, in a cover story on American theme parks, devoted as much space to Africa USA as it did to a new California attraction called Disneyland. And Africa USA made the cover.

John D. Pederson, a Fort Lauderdale real estate investor, opened the 177-acre park in 1953. It was a tropical garden, laced with waterways and populated with hundreds of animals.

Zebras were imported from Kenya and Tanganyika. Later, giraffes, elands, kudus, oryxes and chimpanzees joined them. Within a year, Pederson had transformed a former palmetto patch into one of the largest plant and zoological tropical gardens in the country. Three thousand royal poincianas were planted.

In its heyday, 2,000 visitors a day enjoyed the attractions of Africa USA, which included a train ride through the jungle to a mud and thatch pseudo-African village, staffed by local blacks.

Eventually, the park ran afoul of a familiar Florida problem – the demand for housing and the land to support it.

Neighbors in a new housing development south of Africa USA complained of the noise and traffic. When additional subdivisions were opened to the west, city officials decided the time had come to extend Camino Real to the new residents. Extension required condemnation of some of the parkland.

Early in 1961, an even peskier problem arose. African red ticks were found at the attraction. Health officials threw a quarantine line across the entire southern end of the peninsula. Many of the animals were ordered to be destroyed.

Pederson sold his remaining animals to various zoos and then in October 1961, sold the land to real estate developers in one of the strangest deals ever seen in Boca Raton.

The man to whom Africa USA had been a life-long dream had another: One million dollars, in cash.

The transaction was completed at First Bank of Boca Raton under the watchful eye of Pederson's banker, William M. Stowe, president of the bank.

The cash, by the way, turned out to be a certified check, not a mountain of small bills.

Traces of Africa USA lingered. For a while, peacocks roamed around Camino Gardens in such numbers that the city erected "Peacock Crossing" signs on Camino Real. Souvenir collectors took the signs, and, in time, the peacocks vanished, too.

In 1968, Lion Country Safari, a drive-through African wildlife park, opened on 320 acres in Loxahatchee, west of West Palm Beach, where it remains to this day.

All that remains of Africa USA are its waterways, lush landscaping, and a plentiful, if less exotic, collection of Muscovy ducks.

Zebras at Africa USA. *(Boca Raton Historical Society)*

That Wacky, Upside-Down Sunrise House

Political foes of Sunrise's first elected mayor, John Lomelo, thought he turned the city upside-down. Actually, someone beat him to it.

In 1960, developer Norman Johnson bought 2,650 acres just north of Plantation for a new housing development he was planning. He decided to call it Sunrise Golf Village, taking advantage of an existing golf course adjacent to his property.

But he figured he needed a gimmick to introduce it. And he came up with one that still has people talking.

The idea was born when Johnson, a sports car enthusiast, was driving in Miami. He was suddenly caught in a traffic jam along a street over-populated with automobile dealerships. He assumed there had been an accident. Instead, the tie-up was caused by motorists stopping to gawk at a sales gimmick – an upside-down car on a car dealer's lot.

"Why not an upside-down house?" Johnson asked himself.

So Johnson proceeded to build an upside-down house as a sales model at Sunrise. Furniture was bolted to the floor, a Pontiac convertible was secured to the floor of the carport, and small trees and bushes were planted in an upside-down position.

The furniture, appliances and car obligingly remained in place. Only the plants rebelled. Instead of growing down, they changed position and started reaching toward the sun.

People mobbed the place. Airplane pilots began using the house as a visual check-point when approaching the airport. *Life* magazine sent a photographer and a two-page spread told the nation about Norman Johnson's eye-catching upside-down house.

Best of all, the developer recalls, the gimmick sold houses.

The standing-on-its-head house had cost him roughly 20 percent more to build than a conventional model. Of course, in those days prices were lower. Two-bedroom houses started at $11,300. Three-bedroom models were a little higher, $13,300. Four-bedroom houses were just under $15,000.

When Sunrise Golf Village was incorporated on June 22, 1961, Johnson was appointed its first mayor by Gov. Farris Bryant.

Johnson later developed the Sportatorium on West Hollywood Boulevard, in partnership with the late Steve Calder.

And whatever happened to the upside-down house?

"There was nothing more we could do with it," says Johnson. "We had to destroy it."

The upside-down house. *(Fort Lauderdale Historical Society)*

PART EIGHT

Rooms With a View Historical

Six Dollars and Full Amenities, 1880s Style

About 1880, even before the pioneers had started to call their settlement Palm Beach, a man named Cap Dimick decided to boost the family income by entertaining tourists and fishing parties.

Dimick had a home on Lake Worth surrounded by coconut palms and orange and banana trees. He converted it into an inn by adding eight rooms. He was so successful that subsequent add-ons eventually enlarged his Cocoanut Grove House into a 50-room hostelry.

Guests paid six dollars per person per day for a room, three meals and all the oranges and bananas they could pick. They also had the use of a catboat and a rowboat.

To reach the Cocoanut Grove House, guests traveled as far south as Jupiter via Indian River steamer, then took a covered wagon to the north shore of Lake Worth. This changed in 1888, when the famed "Celestial Railroad" began serving the area.

Five years later, in 1893, railroad tycoon Henry Flagler arrived in Palm Beach with plans to build the world's largest resort hotel. Cap figured the day of his little 50-room hostelry was over. He sold the Cocoanut Grove House to Commodore C.J. Clarke, who in turn rented it to Flagler. It was used to house the workers who were building the Royal Poinciana Hotel.

A year later the Cocoanut Grove House caught fire and burned to the ground. It was truly the end of an era. Palm Beach no longer belonged to its early founders.

But it was not the end of the resourceful Cap Dimick. In turn, he became president of the lake country's first bank, Palm Beach's first mayor and a state senator. A statue of him still stands at the Royal Park Bridge entrance to Palm Beach.

Cocoanut Grove House, ca. 1890. *(Historical Society of Palm Beach County)*

The Elite Roughed It at the Shultz Hotel

Guests of George Shultz, a pioneer Florida innkeeper, had to rough it. But they didn't complain.

Shultz owned a ramshackle Civil War army barracks perched over a bay off Fort Myers. Somehow he managed to convince rich and famous people that his shack was one of the "in" places of the sporting world.

Among the titans he lured there were President Grover Cleveland, inventor Thomas Edison, Hugh O'Neill (whose New York department store had become by 1890 the world's largest), Scotland's Duke of Sutherland, and John Jameson, the Irish whiskey distiller.

As any good hotelier would, Shultz plugged up the unsightly bullet holes left over from the war. He exterminated the rats and the snakes, always bad for business.

His dining room was a delight. Superb meals were cooked at first by his wife, later by a French chef.

The view from the Shultz Hotel, later called the Tarpon House, was magnificent. Guests could gaze out from Punta Rassa (now a part of Fort Myers) over the fish-filled waters of San Carlos Bay toward Sanibel and Estero islands.

Instead of deriding him for not painting the place, Shultz's guests praised him for not tampering with its primitive charms. Instead of calling the hotel rundown, they called it unique.

Shultz didn't start out to be an innkeeper. A native of Newark, New Jersey, he had come to Fort Myers in 1869 as head of a crew laying cable for the International Ocean Telegraph Company. His telegraph office was a curtained-off area of the barracks.

In those days, Punta Rassa was a port for shipping cattle to Havana. Cowboys who slept underneath the building suggested George rent them inside space so they could escape the mosquitoes. So began his hotel career.

Shultz continued using his telegraph, adding a touch that particularly appealed to Wall Street wheeler-dealers. With George's nimble telegrapher's fingers, they could instantly buy and sell stocks from the Tarpon House. He kept them happy until the place burned down in 1906.

The Shultz Hotel at Punta Rassa in the 1890s. *(Florida Photographic Archives)*

Survivors Danced After Dinner at the Royal Poinciana

In its time, Henry Flagler's Royal Poinciana Hotel was the largest in the world. Humorist Ring Lardner claimed the distance from one end of the dining room to the other was a "toll call."

The main dining hall at the belle of Palm Beach luxury hotels could seat 1,600 people. A look at the menu for February 22, 1900, the night of the annual Washington's Birthday Ball, indicates that you might have needed 1,600 people to consume the enormous bounty Flagler's 160 cooks lavished upon the privileged souls who partook of his hospitality. Head waiter Joseph McLane supervised a staff of 32 assistants and 500 waiters.

Meals were included in the price of the room, $38 a day, a sizable sum at the turn of the century. By 1914, room rates had risen to $80 a day.

The Royal Poinciana started you off with canapes, followed by Blue Point oysters, then a choice of three soups and five fancy items, ranging from caviar to brandied peaches.

At that point you enjoyed the fish dish, either shad or smelts, with potatoes Julienne and sliced cucumbers.

Having already consumed the equivalent of a full meal by today's standards, the Poinciana guest confronted the meat course, a selection of ten, including terrapin, chicken, duck, turkey, filet of beef, prime rib, lamb, and even a spaghetti dish. Nine vegetable dishes were yours for the choosing.

After the main course, the choices became downright sinful: 19 desserts, ranging from pies and ice cream to eclairs, a plum pudding with brandy sauce, eight kinds of fruit and five different cheeses.

After the overstuffed guests waddled from their tables, the dining room was cleared to make way for the ball. Apparently anxious for its guests to dance away the huge meal, the hotel employed two full orchestras, so there was never a break in the music. Champagne flowed freely.

At one o'clock the ball ended. Now it was time for a "stand-up supper." This consisted of consomme, almonds, olives, roast squab, sandwiches, capon, quail, Florida lobster, salads, ice cream and cakes.

The next day the hotel closed. In the early days of Palm Beach the "season" lasted just two months. Maybe the guests couldn't stand another month of the Poinciana's rich fare.

Portion of the dining hall at the Royal Poinciana Hotel, early 1900s. (*Henry Morrison Flagler Museum*)

Offering Whiskey, Gambling and Deer

Wayfarers heading to Key West on U.S. 1 used to see an imposing, two-story wooden building to their left as they cruised across Big Pine Key. It was called Big Pine Inn.

You could stop for the night; the inn had 12 rooms, renting for eight dollars a night as recently as the 1960s. Or you could have a drink or a meal. The turtle steak was superb.

That all changed in the early morning hours of December 17, 1978. After more than 70 years, the inn's Dade County pine had simply dried out. Fire broke out and the Lower Keys lost a memorable landmark.

Mrs. Gussie Zeigner started construction of the inn in 1906, before Henry Flagler's railroad reached the area. The building materials – pine and cypress – had to be shipped in by boat. Once the crew went on strike and Gussie unloaded the boards herself.

After completion, the inn welcomed many of the railroad's executives, including Flagler. At one time, the railroad's ticket window was located in the inn. Later it would also house the local Post Office.

It became a gathering place of note, comfortable even in the hot Keys summers thanks to its high ceiling fans. Author James McLendon wrote: "During the '20s and '30s many a good time was had at the inn. Here bonded bootleg whiskey, good meals and gambling would relieve you of your money in every socially accepted way."

The inn's popularity increased further when Flagler's roadbed became the foundation for U.S. 1 after the 1935 hurricane demolished the tracks. From the inn's windows guests could see tiny Key deer, an endangered species found principally in Big Pine.

Then came the fire. Where the famous Big Pine Inn once stood, a bank building has now arisen.

Big Pine Inn, late 1920s. *(Monroe County Public Library)*

Hillsboro's "Big Diamond" in the Sky

From the moment the big kerosene lamp was lighted in March, 1907, it brought an important distinction to the Hillsboro Lighthouse.

The brilliant light, beamed toward seafarers near the Hillsboro Inlet, made it the most powerful lighthouse in the United States. And none too soon.

The waters off the inlet were treacherous, particularly for southbound ships, which tended to hug the shoreline to avoid the northward tug of the Gulf Stream.

Ships risked a deadly encounter with the north end of the Florida Reef, which lies just south of the inlet. The reef's rocky shoals could rip holes in boats' bottoms.

Over the years, the reef had claimed many victims. The Spanish brig *Formento* sank in 1848 near the inlet, its treasure salvaged soon after. Just before the Civil War, the American barkentine *Thales*, an Africa-bound slave ship, sank and was salvaged by Seminoles led by Chief Tiger Tail. And on May 27, 1900, the 325-foot steamer *Copenhagen*, bound for Havana with a cargo of coal, ran aground.

The light was needed, too, to fill the gap between lighthouses along the southeast Florida coast. Hillsboro was roughly halfway between lights at Fowey Rocks in Biscayne Bay and the Jupiter Inlet.

The Hillsboro Lighthouse's all-steel skeleton towered 136 feet. It took two years for the Champion Bridge Company, of Wilmington, Ohio, to complete construction of the tower. The lighthouse was called Big Diamond because of its unusual lens, which consisted of glass prisms arranged in circular fashion. The lens, built in Paris, cost $7,250.

The first lighthouse keeper was Alfred Berghill, who served for four years. He was succeeded by Thomas Knight, whose father and grandfather before him were keepers of the Cape Canaveral Lighthouse. Tom's brother was Cap Knight who became famous later for Cap's Place restaurant, across the Intracoastal Waterway from the light.

In the early days, three men were needed to operate the station. Their job was to wind the lens-rotation machinery every half-hour by crank to keep the signal revolving from one hour before dusk to one hour after after sunrise.

Roughly twice a year, a schooner out of Charleston, S.C., would anchor offshore and send in a shallow-draft boat bringing kerosene and other supplies.

In 1920, electricity replaced kerosene, further strengthening the power of the beam. During the '20s, much of the inlet's traffic consisted of rum-running boats from

The Hillsboro Lighthouse. *(Fort Lauderdale Historical Society)*

Nassau and Havana. Today, drug smugglers are likely to pass through the inlet.

The Big Diamond's eye has blinked only once – when the 1926 hurricane briefly extinguished its light. Today the lighthouse, listed in the National Register of Historic Places, is a picturesque landmark. It was automated in the 1960s, and the lighthouse keeper is now a Coast Guardsman, making sure the old diamond still shines.

Behind the Pink Wall

Today it's called Wildflower, a popular, happy hour night-time restaurant and nightclub on the east bank of the Intracoastal Waterway, just north of Palmetto Park Road in Boca Raton. In years past, it was Palmetto Park Plantation and, later, Casa Rosa, the Pink House.

More than 80 years ago, Harley Gates, a successful Vermont realtor, came to Boca Raton, seeking relief for his asthma. When his condition improved, thanks to the South Florida climate, Gates bought five acres on the waterway for $225.

He returned to Vermont and persuaded his fiancee, Harriette, to marry him and move to Boca. Harley and Harriette made their first home a West Indian-style bungalow made of cement blocks.

Gates added 26 more acres to the original five, which gave him a sizeable holding, and on this land he planted native and exotic fruits, and changed the name to Palmetto Park Plantation. The plantation was an early Boca showplace, drawing many visitors, including Seminole Indians, from the surrounding country.

Harley and Harriette and their children, Imogene Alice and Buddy (Harley Jr.), continued to live in the house even after they sold it to Canadian Stan Harris in 1923.

Harris added two more rooms and a tower, built a wall along Palmetto Park Road, painted the whole place pink and renamed it Casa Rosa – Pink House.

"I used to go up to the tower and just sit with my peanut butter and my books," recalls Imogene Alice. "You could look out on the ocean. I remember, too, we used to sit on the wall and sing country songs."

Later, Imogene Alice Gates blossomed into quite a beauty who performed on the stage and in elegant supper clubs as Diane DeLys. Now she is known as Diane Gates Benedetto. Buddy took the opposite course from his father and returned to Vermont where he works as a coin dealer.

After Stan Harris, Casa Rosa went through several hands. It was bought by an Italian family named Marrafino, but their plan to build a restaurant on the site never materialized after they tore the old house down in 1967 – all, that is, except the pink wall.

The pink wall is still there. When its next owner, Mrs. G.E. Goldhahn, built Wildflower in 1980, she insisted the old wall be retained as a legacy of Boca Raton's past.

Casa Rosa, the Pink House. (*Boca Raton Historical Society*)

A House With Humor

The Bartlett Estate on Fort Lauderdale's beach is the most valuable property owned by any state historic preservation society in America. Its main building, Bonnet House, has been the focus of serious restoration work for many years.

Yet Bonnet House isn't a place for stuffy historians. "This is the only great house I've ever known with a sense of humor," said Carl Weinhardt, director of the Bonnet House until his death in 1985. "The whole thing is tongue-in-cheek, displaying a sophisticated and subtle humor that pervaded the lives of its owners."

How does a house come by a sense of humor? In this case it was built into the residence by a Chicago artist named Frederic Clay Bartlett.

Bartlett married Helen Louise Birch, whose father, wealthy Chicago attorney Hugh Taylor Birch, owned most of Fort Lauderdale's beach. For a wedding present he gave the newlyweds a "house lot" on the beach.

How big a lot?

"Oh, about as far as you can swing a cat," said Birch.

Barlett must have had a good swing. The lot turned out to be 35 acres with 700 feet of ocean front.

Bartlett built Bonnet House in 1920-21, making it a huge painting studio. Because it was designed to be lived in, not to impress people, it reflects the whimsy of its owners. (The home was named after the bonnet lily, found in a pond on the property.)

Frederic's murals decorate ceilings and walls. There are animals from antique carousels: a lifesize ostrich, a giraffe, a lion and a tiger.

When Helen Birch died in 1926, three-fifths of the ownership of the tract was returned to her father. When Bartlett married Evelyn Fortune five years later, he transferred the rest of it to Birch. In 1939, Birch gave the whole thing back to Bartlett for one dollar.

Frederic Bartlett died in 1953. His widow gave the estate – valued at roughly $35 million – to the Florida Trust for Historic Preservation. For seven months of the year the Bonnet House is open to the public for scheduled tours and for weddings.

The Bonnet House. *(Fort Lauderdale Historical Society)*

Boca Ratone by the Sea

Today a huge hotel, the Boca Beach Club, sits on the north side of the Boca Raton Inlet. Built by the Arvida Corporation in 1980 at a cost of some twenty million dollars the hotel contains 213 rooms.

Big as the hotel looks, it is vastly smaller than the 1,000-room hotel Addison Mizner had dreamed of building in the same location, but then again, size is relative. The Beach Club is far bigger than the picturesque little dance hall/filling station called Boca Ratone by the Sea that sat on the spot before 1925.

Even old-timers remember little about Boca Ratone by the Sea, except that it was the nearest thing to an all-purpose beach facility the young settlement had ever seen. In addition to its dance hall and gas pumps, it functioned as a bar and lounge, a good place to buy fishing tackle or Michelin tires, and as home for a man named Griffin, the bridgetender at the bridge over the inlet. Some even called Boca Ratone by the Sea "Grif's Place."

Then, in 1925, Mizner came to Boca Raton. Among the potential building sites considered by the master architect was the land on the north side of the inlet.

Mizner had a great dream for the beachfront location, a 1,000-, possibly even a 2,000-room hotel to be called Castillo del Rey, the Castle of the King. The Ritz-Carlton hotel people became interested in the project and it seemed to be moving right along. From the daybook of Karl Riddle, Mizner's chief engineer, was this entry, dated October 21, 1925: "...also to prepare notes to tenant to vacate Dance Hall at Ritz-Carlton site."

Riddle remembers nothing about Boca Ratone by the Sea. He was used to dealing with much more elaborate structures.

When the bust came in 1926, Mizner's dreams for the north side of the inlet died along with the local economy. Later, Clarence Geist, who took over Mizner's bankrupt properties, had the inlet redredged a little to the north of its former location.

Then in the 1950s, the spot caught the eye of one Arthur Vining Davis, the man whose name and vast land holdings would become Arvida. By then, Boca Ratone by the Sea, had become only a vague memory, preserved in a few old photographs.

Boca Ratone by the Sea. *(Boca Raton Historical Society)*

178

Hot Times at the Pompano Casino

The old Pompano Casino had everything – locker rooms and showers for daytime bathers and, at night, a dance hall complete with orchestra.

The casino, or as it was more formally known, the Pompano Beach Bathing Pavilion and Dance Casino, was built in the 1920s, just south of the spot where Atlantic Boulevard meets the beach. Today, the Ever April Apartments complex occupies the site.

For its time the casino was a "biggie." The City of Pompano appropriated $15,000 for its construction and hired a fancy Fort Lauderdale architect, C. Hobart Sherwood, to come up with an appropriately Spanish-style design. One of the casino's early boosters called it "one of the most complete structures of its kind between Palm Beach and Miami."

Music was furnished by the Johnson-Brinson Orchestra. Its pianist was Ora Johnson, who taught piano in town. The violin was played by Mrs. Vivian Brinson and the drums by her husband.

Dances were well attended and well chaperoned. This, however, did not prevent frequent trips to the moonshine jug and the occasional fist fight. "Just about the liveliest events in town," said an early account.

By the early '50s, however, the casino's glories had faded. In April, 1953, the city leased the building to the Pompano Beach Elks Lodge, which had been organized the year before. The Elks invested heavily in fixtures and equipment, and were well on their way to putting the building back in shape when disaster struck.

On Saturday night, November 27, 1954, the Elks held their annual Thanksgiving dance. At 2:10 a.m. Sunday morning they closed up the place and headed for home.

At 5:10, a police officer discovered fire and promptly sounded the alarm. It was already too late. The cypress and pine planking was burning rapidly, and heat burst the whiskey bottles, further fueling the flames.

It was a particularly trying day for Ed Haynie. As Exalted Ruler of the Elks Lodge 1898, he surveyed the loss of $18,000 in Elks' fixtures, equipment and whiskey. And, wearing another hat, he had cause, as the mayor of Pompano Beach, to lament the loss of a city building valued at $25,000.

The next years the Elks built a lodge of their own at 2300 NE 10th Street. They occupied it for nearly three decades before moving into a handsome new $1.3 million building at 700 NE 10th Street.

Pompano Casino. *(Pompano Beach Public Library)*

Miami's Ellis Island

Today it towers over downtown Miami's Biscayne Boulevard, a hollow echo of its colorful past.

It started life as one of America's finest newspaper buildings, and later earned the title of Freedom Tower when it served as headquarters for processing some 400,000 Cuban refugees.

The formal opening of the Miami News Tower on July 26, 1925, was observed by a noteworthy feat: the publication of the largest-ever single issue of a newspaper to that time: 504 pages, 1,200 stories, 1,000 photos, 22 sections. It took 50 carloads of newsprint to publish the edition, which held the record for 40 years until 1965, when *The New York Times* surpassed it with a 946-pager.

In the mid-1920s, the Florida land boom was raging so chaotically that the *Miami Daily News* was the fifth biggest paper in the country. Times have changed: today, it's not even the fifth largest in Florida.

The owner of the *News* was Gov. James M. Cox, governor of Ohio for three terms and in 1920 the Democratic presidential candidate. His running mate in the election was Franklin D. Roosevelt, who would be heard from again. Cox decided that his paper's prosperity called for a monumental new building.

Since boomtime Miami's ruling architecture was Mediterranean-style, the governor concluded that true eminence would be achieved by a design based on the world-famous Giralda Tower in Seville, Spain. It was a popular choice. At the time two other Giralda-type towers were going up – the Miami Biltmore Hotel in Coral Gables and the Roney Plaza on Miami Beach.

Governor Cox also decided that the proper way for a newspaper to recognize a move to a new building was by a special edition. His Dayton, Ohio *Daily News* had already cranked out a huge edition of 250 pages in November 1923. Cox was apparently into big special issues.

Eleanor Bisbee was editor of the garguantuan, opening-day edition. It took her and her staff a year to pull the issue together, but the end result was well received. So well, in fact, that the editions were soon selling for as much as $20 apiece on the streets. The edition also marked a freedom of sorts for Bisbee, who had worked her way out of a job.

In the 1960s, Freedom Tower would make its mark as the Miami equivalent of New York's Ellis Island – the place where thousands of Cuban refugees began new lives in a country free of political oppression.

Freedom Tower, designated a historic structure by both the City of Miami and the federal government, is being preserved as part of a large office project.

Miami's Freedom Tower. (*Nicholas Von Staden, Sunshine Magazine*)

From Millionaire's School to Millionaires' Club

Bert Malcolm knew a boom when he saw one. Bert, an upwardly mobile school teacher, came to Miami in 1907 after graduating from Yale. He taught at the Lake Placid School for Boys in Coconut Grove and wound up owning the school.

In the 1920s, the energetic Malcolm bought 1,000 feet of ocean-front property just north of the Hillsboro Inlet. He built a second Lake Placid School, and in 1923 he started bringing in rich boys to study in the shadow of the Hillsboro Light.

Malcolm had one serious problem: He wasn't bringing in enough rich boys.

After two struggling years, Bert gazed out on the South Florida land boom and concluded that there might be a more profitable way to use two large buildings nestled on the sandy beaches of the Atlantic.

Malcom remodeled his school buildings into Broward County's first luxury resort. Instead of millionaires' boys, he went after the millionaires themselves. In the fall of 1925, he opened the Hillsboro Club.

The club could accommodate only 60 guests, which worked to Bert's long-term advantage. Because the available space was well below the demand, his club promptly gained the most enviable of all images. It became "exclusive," and remains that way to this day.

Malcolm expanded it to accommodate more than 200 guests, added tennis courts and a mini-golf course, but he always kept it exclusive. By incorporating as a club rather than a hotel, he could screen out applicants. Furthermore, to protect the privacy of his often-famous guests, he surrounded his property with a fence.

All during the Depression his club continued to operate at a profit.

The Lake Placid School for millionare boys is long gone, but part of its name lives on in a lagoon just west of the club. It's called Lake Placid.

Hillsboro Club, Hillsboro Lighthouse at left. *(Fort Lauderdale Historical Society)*

The "Immortal" Hotel of Delray Beach

Albert T. Repp came up with a good idea for immortalizing his name. The only trouble was it didn't work.

At the height of the Florida land boom in 1925, hotel-building was a popular pastime in Delray. That was the year E.H. Scott built the Seacrest and Henry J. Sterling threw up the Casa Del-Ray. Repp was pushing hard to complete his 118-room, three-story "grand hotel" at the corner of Atlantic Avenue and U.S. 1.

On March 1, 1926, the Alterep Hotel opened for business. The ambitious Repp had gone first-class, including furnishings from John Wanamaker's famed Philadelphia department store, not far from Repp's roots in the South Jersey town of Glassboro.

Unfortunately, 1926 was the year the real estate boom collapsed. The bust was followed by the killer hurricane of 1926 and then by the Great Depression. Albert Repp's hotel veered into bankruptcy.

In 1935, the hotel was bought by the Boughtons, a family of experienced hoteliers whose holdings were in Atlantic City and Cape May, New Jersey. Repp had lost his hotel. Now he lost his name, too. The new owners, understandably, renamed it the Colony, which they also applied to a hotel they owned in Kennebunkport, Maine.

Ironically, Repp's boomtime hotel proved to have staying power. The Seacrest and the Casa Del-Ray are long since gone. But the Colony, originally built as a monument to Al T. Repp, is still going strong over six decades after it first opened its doors in the Roaring Twenties.

The Alterep Hotel, 1926. *(Delray Beach Historical Society)*

Only the Bell Remains

Today, the Broward County Courthouse stands as an undistinguished multi-story structure just south of downtown Fort Lauderdale. It could easily pass for any other office building.

There was a time, though, when the courthouse told the people of Broward loud and clear that here was the seat of government, bristling with authority and power. Law-breakers, beware! Delinquent taxpayers, cringe in fear!

From 1928, when it was completed, until 1960, when the structure was radically changed, it stood at the corner of SE 6th Street and 3rd Avenue as an impressive example of South Florida architecture, complete with tile roof, tower and a bell that gonged on the half-hour.

It was not the county's first courthouse, however. When Broward was created in 1915, cut mostly from Dade but partly from Palm Beach, the county commissioners authorized the purchase of an old school building at the corner of Andrews Avenue and SE 5th Street.

In 1926, the county decided to build a bigger and better courthouse. Land at the present site was bought for $125,000. Another $375,000 went into the construction of a building worthy of an up-and-coming county.

The tower soared to a height of 90 feet above street level, and contained a two-bedroom apartment for the jailer. Above his apartment hung the tower's large bronze bell. When he wasn't busy tending to his prisoners, the jailer had the added duty of keeping the clanging bell wound, a particularly galling task for one who had to sleep under a bell so loud that it could be heard throughout most of Fort Lauderdale.

In 1947 and 1956, additions were made to the courthouse. In 1960, when the Frank Rooney Construction Company razed the tower, workers found it inhabited by thousands of bees, cockroaches and pigeons.

The old bell doesn't ring anymore, but it's still around. You can see it today in the lobby of the courthouse.

Broward County Courthouse, ca. 1930. *(Fort Lauderdale Historical Society)*

One Man is an Island

On Craig Key nothing was quite as it seemed. Poor Old Craig wasn't exactly poor, and Poor Old Craig's Hotel wasn't exactly operated as a home for the indigent.

Furthermore, Craig wasn't exactly a key; it was just a good-sized landfill, dating back to Florida Keys railroad construction in the early 1900s. And Craig wasn't really a town. It had just one full-time resident – Roland Craig.

But Craig had a post office. It was granted to the one-man town, the story goes, to make it easier for an important national figure to pick up his mail when cruising through the Keys. The visitor was an enthusiastic fisherman named Herbert Hoover, president from 1929 to 1933.

Roland Craig, who came to Florida from Ohio, was particularly proud of President Hoover's patronage. His fishing lodge, located just above Long Key, catered to a few wealthy sportsmen who felt the unimpressive look of Poor Old Craig's Hotel guaranteed an obscure hideaway.

Inside, the lodge was a good deal less stark. Its six rooms were attractively decorated. Food was good, including what was claimed to be "the best key lime pie in the Keys."

Craig's fiefdom also included Craig's Store, which sold groceries, beer, fishing tackle and water, five cents a gallon; Craig's Bar, offering beer, wine, whiskey, poker, craps and slot machines, around the clock; Craig's Service Station; and Craig's Marina.

Craig also invested with considerable success in Keys land. He used to show up at Miami casinos, his pockets bulging with cash, cheerfully announcing, "Here comes Poor Old Craig."

Hurricane Donna in 1960 destroyed five of the seven buildings on Craig Key. The Florida State Road Department, which leased the land to Craig, ordered the other two demolished, then reclaimed the fill.

When Craig went back to Miami, Keys pioneer Del Layton had the post office moved to his nearby town, Layton, on Long Key. At first the federal government made him use the name "Craig Post Office" and the road department compounded the insult by erecting "Craig" signs on either end of the mile-long village of Layton.

"Funny thing about those road signs," recalled Layton. "They kept disappearing."

So did the identity of Craig, who died a few years ago. In time the U.S. government renamed its postal outlet "Long Key Post Office" and Del's town became Layton, not Craig.

Poor Old Craig.

Poor Old Craig's Hotel. *(Monroe County Public Library)*

The Floating Hotel That Survived Three Wars

From the start, Fort Lauderdale's floating hotel was a hit.

Docked on the east side of the Intracoastal Waterway near today's Swimming Hall of Fame, she proved to be an attractive Depression-era novelty for tourists and locals alike.

Built in 1895 as a warship, the 259-foot *Amphitrite* had seen naval action in two wars – at San Juan, Puerto Rico, during the Spanish-American War and in New York Harbor during World War I, where she maintained torpedo nets. In 1931, she was moved to Fort Lauderdale and moored just a block away from the ocean.

The rates for the *Amphitrite's* 75 rooms were $4.50-$6 a day for the American Plan and $2.50-$3.50 for the European Plan.

Food was also reasonable. A March 1931, menu offered a dinner which included filet mignon and fricassee of chicken, fish appetizer, vegetable, soup, salad and dessert, all for $1.25.

For four years, the *Amphitrite* prospered. Then in September 1935, she floated away under the prodding of a major hurricane, and wound up in a cove off Idlewyld, at SE 26th Avenue and Las Olas Boulevard. The owners decided to stay in the Las Olas area, and that's when the troubles started.

Claiming that the old floater was a public nuisance, the Idlewyld-Riviera Corporation petitioned the courts to have her removed. The State Board of Health backed the petition. For the next seven years, the ship was caught in the crossfire between warring factions.

Then came World War II and a decision from Washington to press the old warship into service again. One night in July 1942, she was quietly towed out of town. However, Washington didn't know what to do with the old relic, and she spent the duration tucked away in anchorage at Elizabeth City, North Carolina.

After the war, she enjoyed one more moment of glory. Bethlehem Steel used the ship as a floating work camp during the construction of the huge Chesapeake Bay Bridge.

In 1951, however, the *Amphitrite* finally died a predictable death, and her hull of Swedish iron wound up as scrap metal.

The floating *Amphitrite* Hotel. *(Fort Lauderdale Historical Society)*

The Kid, the Tycoon and the Temple

Moe Katz was 36, but Sam Lerner always insisted on calling him "kid". It didn't bother Moe one bit – and with good reason.

Katz, a Brooklyn native, had first arrived in Fort Lauderdale in 1923 to sell real estate. At the time, there were only seven Jewish families in town, but by the mid-1930s, there were enough to build a modest temple. Katz became a leading force in making it happen.

One lucky day in 1936, Sam Lerner and his 85-year-old father, Charles, who had founded the Lerner chain of retail stores, were visiting Fort Lauderdale, checking on the construction of a new store. By chance, they spotted another construction site on South Andrews Avenue, with a sign proclaiming that it would be the future Temple Emanu-El. The Lerners sought out Moe Katz.

"Kid, did you ever build a temple before?" asked Sam. "I can see you don't know what you're doing. But my father thinks any kid with guts enough to try it ought to have help."

Sam produced a check for $1,000 to compensate Katz for tearing up the existing foundation and replacing it with one for a temple three times larger. The new cost rose to $50,000 – steep for a building fund of only $4,000.

"Don't worry about it," Sam said to Theodore Meyer, who was asked to draw up new plans. "My father wants to help this kid and he will."

Soon afterward, the Lerners checked into the Hollywood Beach Hotel, a popular wintering spot for Jewish tourists. Sam introduced Moe around to the well-heeled visitors in his usual breezy way. "This kid is building a temple in Fort Lauderdale and he needs help."

And help he got.

Not only did Sam raise money for the temple, but he also built a continuing contributors list.

"Before you open the temple, you must have cards printed to read 'Honorary Member of Temple Emanu-El,' " Sam instructed Moe. "Each contributor who gave $25 or more must receive one with an invitation for the opening. And each year send them a bill for $50."

With such sound fiscal planning, the new temple was completed in September 1937. Moe Katz would serve as its president for ten years.

During the inaugural service, the congregation was reminded of the first Jewish services ever held in Fort Lauderdale, in temporary quarters on Las Olas Boulevard. It was on a gusty night in September 1926; a few hours later, a killer hurricane came ashore and blew away the second floor.

After that, Sam and the Kid figured they were due for a run of good luck.

Temple Emanu-El. *(Fort Lauderdale Historical Society)*

A Cabana at the Escape, $26 for the Summer

They were quiet times on Fort Lauderdale Beach, those days just after World War II. No Strip, no throngs of Spring Breakers, only three hotels on the entire beach.

Bob Gill and his partner, Fred Franke, two transplanted Chicagoans, figured it was time for one more. They decided to call it the Escape, a place to get away from it all.

"People come to Florida to escape regulations and restrictions," explained Franke. "What they want most is relaxation and informality. We will encourage our guests to eat breakfast or lunch on the patio in their bathing suits." An obvious comment by today's standards, but remember this was 40 years ago.

The mood was tropical: Rattan furniture, lushly landscaped courtyards and a cocktail lounge called the Malayan Room. It was embellished by a massive South Seas mural painted by a well-known local artist of the time, John DeGroot.

The Escape's 34-year career as a hotel kicked off at a perfect time, New Year's Eve, 1949, the dawn of the first postwar decade.

"People were trying to recover from the war," recalls architect Clinton Gamble. He was one of the regulars at the Escape, destined to establish itself quickly as the "in" place for present and future Fort Lauderdale establishment types.

In its first year, future mayor Bob Cox went there "for the swimming," a big selling point since the Escape was the first hotel on the beach to offer a pool. Other hotels had figured that the nearby ocean was all the water they needed.

"You could rent a cabana at the Escape for $26 for the entire summer," remembers Cox. "And that was all I could afford at the time."

In 1961, bestselling novelist Robert Ruark discovered the Escape and in one of his widely-syndicated columns brought it and a singer/pianist named Ken Watkins a fleeting taste of fame.

Just back from Spain, the globe-trotting author of *Something of Value* needed a quiet place to complete a second novel about Africa titled *Uhuru*.

At one time, Ruark's secretary had been Myrtle "Andy" Anderson. She had later moved to Fort Lauderdale to pursue a real estate career, and she now lined up a quiet suite at the Escape for Ruark. In the evenings the author often dropped by a lounge called the Nassau Bar, where Ken Watkins played. In a glowing column run in some 400 newspapers Ruark wrote:

"You do not expect to find a man like Kenny Watkins outside of Tangier or some sleepy South Sea backwater, where he might have gone to forget some long-buried tragedy...

"The man has the greatest gift for the invocation of nostalgia that I have ever run across...His voice brings

The Escape Hotel decorated for a Christmas Past.
(Gene Hyde Collection, Fort Lauderdale Historical Society)

back the memory of the girl that got away...And close by the piano you can suddenly see the trickle of tears on a girl's face, or a man bite his lip, or a hand steal out and seize another hand.

"It is really most remarkable to find such a completely old-fashioned romantic baladeer in Fort Lauderdale, Florida."

At a hotel which featured musical entertainment from the start, Watkins proved to be the most durable and most popular of all the Escape's entertainers.

"The Escape was strictly for townspeople, except for the Chicagoans Bob Gill used to attract," recalls Watkins, who lives now in semi-retirement in Nashville, North Carolina. "I still remember the Bachelor's Club on Fridays and Saturdays. I never did know what all was going on. Next thing I knew, these fellows were Fort Lauderdale's top city officials, community leaders and bankers. They were a nice bunch of guys."

For school dances the Escape sometimes engaged the services of a popular local group from Fort Lauderdale High School, known in the trade as Bill Markham and

Bonanza Room entertainers. *(Gene Hyde Collection, Fort Lauderdale Historical Society)*

the Jesters. People today know Bill Markham as their friendly, hometown tax assessor, but from 1955 to 1958 he was better known as a lead singer, liable with minimal encouragement to break into such classics as *Hound Dog* and *Heartbreak Hotel*.

"We were paid five dollars a night apiece," recalls Markham. "By the time I went away to college we were getting as much as $50-60 for our four-man group. It was a dancing era. Everybody came to dance."

In 1984, the Escape ceased to operate as a resort hotel. Jerome Vogel, who had purchased the 133-room complex, decided the time had come to convert it into a retirement hotel, or as he put it "a Club Med for the octogenarians."

When it reopened as Tiffany House, the man who represented the City of Fort Lauderdale as official ribbon-cutter was a man whose memories of the Escape went back to its first year of operation, city commissioner (later mayor) Bob Cox.

189

Down by the Riverside

Preston and John Wells liked deep sea fishing, particularly on the *Caliban*, a Fort Lauderdale charter boat. The brothers could well afford to venture out on the briny as often as they wanted. They had made a fortune in Chicago real estate and Nebraska cattle, and by investing in a company called Quaker Oats.

During their many chases after fish the brothers became close friends with the *Caliban's* mate, Champ Carr, a Missourian named after a famous Missouri senator, Champ Clark. Affable, articulate and ebullient, Carr had a seemingly endless supply of amusing stories.

The Wellses, who had just purchased a small hotel, decided Champ was just the man to run it. The former fisherman proved so successful as manager of the Las Olas Hotel that the brothers decided to get into the business in a big way.

In 1936 they began construction of a three-story, 80-room hotel, designed by Fort Lauderdale's finest architect, Francis Abreu, and built by contractor George Young. The hotel property fronted Las Olas Boulevard and extended all the way to the New River.

The new hotel opened on December 17, 1936. It eventually would become the Riverside Hotel but its first name was the Hotel Champ Carr. Among its first wave of visitors was a DuPont. Later, celebrity guests would include a Californian named Ronald Reagan.

Its first season was so successful that a six-story wing was added the following year, increasing the room total to 125. It was built by another George Young, son of the original contractor.

In 1947, Champ Carr stepped down as manager and the hotel's name was changed to Riverside.

Until 1947, the Riverside was open only from November 1 to May 1. One of its regular guests in earlier years was Edgar A. Guest, the famous poet.

Guest wrote a poem at the hotel on February 27, 1949. He called it "Riverside Shufflers," a paean to the vigorous sport of shuffleboard.

It read, in part:

Oh! here is a most exciting game,
Designed for the blind, the deaf and the lame...
It is even allowed in this friendly strife
To choose for your partner another man's wife.

Hotel Champ Carr in the 1930s. *(Fort Lauderdale Historical Society)*